# 1964–1985 Affinità – Divergenze Fra Il Compagno Togliatti e Noi – Del Conseguimento Della Maggiore Età

# 33 1/3 Global

**33 1/3 Global**, a series related to but independent from **33 1/3**, takes the format of the original series of short, music-based books and brings the focus to music throughout the world. With initial volumes focusing on Japanese and Brazilian music, the series will also include volumes on the popular music of Australia/Oceania, Europe, Africa, the Middle East, and more.

## 33 1/3 Japan

Series Editor: Noriko Manabe

Spanning a range of artists and genres – from the 1970s rock of Happy End to technopop band Yellow Magic Orchestra, the Shibuya-kei of Cornelius, classic anime series *Cowboy Bebop*, J-Pop/EDM hybrid Perfume, and vocaloid star Hatsune Miku – 33 1/3 Japan is a series devoted to in-depth examination of Japanese popular music of the twentieth and twenty-first centuries.

Published Titles:
Supercell's *Supercell* by Keisuke Yamada
*AKB48* by Patrick W. Galbraith and Jason G. Karlin
Yoko Kanno's *Cowboy Bebop Soundtrack* by Rose Bridges
Perfume's *Game* by Patrick St. Michel
Cornelius's *Fantasma* by Martin Roberts
Joe Hisaishi's *My Neighbor Totoro: Soundtrack* by Kunio Hara
Shonen Knife's *Happy Hour* by Brooke McCorkle
Nenes' *Koza Dabasa* by Henry Johnson
Yuming's *The 14th Moon* by Lasse Lehtonen
Toshiko Akiyoshi-Lew Tabackin Big Band's *Kogun* by E. Taylor Atkins
S.O.B.'s *Don't Be Swindle* by Mahon Murphy and Ran Zwigenberg

Forthcoming Titles:
Kohaku Utagassen: The Red and White Song Contest by Shelley Brunt
Yellow Magic Orchestra's *Yellow Magic Orchestra* by Toshiyuki Ohwada

## 33 1/3 Brazil

Series Editor: Jason Stanyek

Covering the genres of samba, tropicália, rock, hip hop, forró, bossa nova, heavy metal, and funk, among others, 33 1/3 Brazil is a series devoted to in-depth examination of the most important Brazilian albums of the twentieth and twenty-first centuries.

Published Titles:
Caetano Veloso's *A Foreign Sound* by Barbara Browning
Tim Maia's *Tim Maia Racional Vols. 1 &2* by Allen Thayer
João Gilberto and Stan Getz's *Getz/Gilberto* by Brian McCann
Gilberto Gil's *Refazenda* by Marc A. Hertzman
Dona Ivone Lara's *Sorriso Negro* by Mila Burns
Milton Nascimento and Lô Borges's *The Corner Club* by Jonathon Grasse
Racionais MCs' *Sobrevivendo no Inferno* by Derek Pardue
Naná Vasconcelos's *Saudades* by Daniel B. Sharp
Chico Buarque's First *Chico Buarque* by Charles A. Perrone

Forthcoming Titles:
Jorge Ben Jor's *África Brasil* by Frederick J. Moehn

## 33 1/3 Europe

Series Editor: Fabian Holt

Spanning a range of artists and genres, 33 1/3 Europe offers engaging accounts of popular and culturally significant albums of Continental Europe and the North Atlantic from the twentieth and twenty-first centuries.

Published Titles:
Darkthrone's *A Blaze in the Northern Sky* by Ross Hagen
Ivo Papazov's *Balkanology* by Carol Silverman
Heiner Müller and Heiner Goebbels's *Wolokolamsker Chaussee* by Philip V. Bohlman
Modeselektor's *Happy Birthday!* by Sean Nye
Mercyful Fate's *Don't Break the Oath* by Henrik Marstal

Bea Playa's *I'll Be Your Plaything* by Anna Szemere and András Rónai
Various Artists' *DJs do Guetto* by Richard Elliott
Czesław Niemen's *Niemen Enigmatic* by Ewa Mazierska and Mariusz Gradowski
Massada's *Astaganaga* by Lutgard Mutsaers
Los Rodriguez's *Sin Documentos* by Fernán del Val and Héctor Fouce
Édith Piaf's *Récital 1961* by David Looseley
Nuovo Canzoniere Italiano's *Bella Ciao* by Jacopo Tomatis
Iannis Xenakis's *Persepolis* by Aram Yardumian
Vopli Vidopliassova's *Tantsi* by Maria Sonevytsky
Amália Rodrigues's *Amália at the Olympia* by Lila Ellen Gray
Ardit Gjebrea's *Projekt Jon* by Nicholas Tochka
Aqua's *Aquarium* by C.C. McKee
J.M.K.E.'s *To the Cold Land* by Brigitta Davidjants
Taco Hemingway's *Jarmark* by Kamila Rymajdo
Einstürzende Neubauten's *Kollaps* by Melle Jan Kromhout and Jan Nieuwenhuis
CCCP – FEDELI ALLA LINEA's *Affinità – Divergenze Fra il Compagno Togliatti e Noi* by Giacomo Bottà

Forthcoming Titles:
Silly's *Februar* by Michael Rauhut
Sigur Rós' *Ágætis Byrjun* by Tore Størvold

## 33 1/3 Oceania

Series Editors: Jon Stratton (senior editor) and Jon Dale (specializing in books on albums from Aotearoa/New Zealand)

Spanning a range of artists and genres from Australian Indigenous artists to Maori and Pasifika artists, from Aotearoa/New Zealand noise music to Australian rock, and including music from Papua and other Pacific islands, 33 1/3 Oceania offers exciting accounts of albums that illustrate the wide range of music made in the Oceania region.

Published Titles:
John Farnham's *Whispering Jack* by Graeme Turner
The Church's *Starfish* by Chris Gibson

Regurgitator's *Unit* by Lachlan Goold and Lauren Istvandity
Kylie Minogue's *Kylie* by Adrian Renzo and Liz Giuffre
Alastair Riddell's *Space Waltz* by Ian Chapman
Hunters & Collectors's *Human Frailty* by Jon Stratton
The Front Lawn's *Songs from the Front Lawn* by Matthew Bannister
Bic Runga's *Drive* by Henry Johnson
The Dead C's *Clyma est mort* by Darren Jorgensen
Ed Kuepper's *Honey Steel's Gold* by John Encarnacao
Chain's *Toward the Blues* by Peter Beilharz
Hilltop Hoods' *The Calling* by Dianne Rodger
Screamfeeder's *Kitten Licks* by Ben Green and Ian Rogers
The Clean's *Boodle Boodle Boodle* by Geoff Stahl
The Avalanches' *Since I Left You* by Charles Fairchild
John Sangster's *Lord of the Rings Vols. 1–3* by Bruce Johnson
Soundtrack from *Saturday Night Fever* by Clinton Walker
Eyeliner's *BUY NOW* by Michael Brown
TISM's *Machiavelli and the Four Seasons* by Tyler Jenke
Crowded House's *Together Alone* by Barnaby Smith
silverchair's *Frogstomp* by Jay Daniel Thompson
Various Artists' *Truckload of Sky: The Lost Songs of David McComb* by Glenn D'Cruz
Robert Forster's *Danger in the Past* by Patrick Chapman
Tame Impala's *Currents* by Alister Newstead

Forthcoming Titles:
The Triffids' *Born Sandy Devotional* by Christina Ballico
5MMM's *Compilation Album of Adelaide Bands 1980* by Collette Snowden
INXS' *Kick* by Lauren Moxey
Sunnyboys' *Sunnyboys* by Stephen Bruel
The La De Das' *The Happy Prince* by John Tebbutt
Gary Shearston's *Dingo* by Peter Mills
Kate Ceberano's *Brave* by Panizza Allmark
Dinah Lee's *Introducing Dinah Lee* by Kimberly Cannady
The Waifs' *Up All Night* by Rebecca Bennison
The Three Out's *Move* by James Gaunt

Split Enz' *Mental Notes* by Michael Lamb
Douglas Lilburn's *Complete Electro-Acoustic Works* by Bruce Russell
Savage Garden's *Affirmation* by Pat O'Grady
Dick Diver's *Calendar Days* by Mitch Ryan

## 33 1/3 South Asia

Series Editor: Natalie Sarrazin

From the films of Bollywood and Lollywood, to home-grown *bhangra* hip-hop, Hindu devotional pop and Sufi rock, Sri Lankan rap, Indo jazz and disco, new-wave electronica, and diasporic Asian Underground scene, 33 1/3 South Asia takes readers on a sonically diverse journey through the most significant soundtracks and albums from the twentieth and twenty-first centuries.

Published Titles:
*Dil Chahta Hai* Soundtrack by Jayson Beaster-Jones
Lata Mangeshkar's *My Favourites, Volume 2* by Anirudha Bhattacharjee and Chandrashekhar Rao
*Coke Studio* (Season 14) by Rakae Rehman Jamil and Khadija Muzaffar

## 33 1/3 Africa

Series Editor: Michael Veal

33 1/3 Africa is a series of books on canonical, album-length works of African music including traditional music, experimental music, and, with particular emphasis, popular music. Academic and journalistic writing results in sophisticated, nuanced, and accessible narratives on African music.

Published Titles:
Fela Anikulapo-Kuti's *Sorrow Tears and Blood* by Stephanie Shonekan

Forthcoming Titles:
Cesária Évora's *Miss Perfumado* by Jacqueline Georgis
Paul Simon's *Graceland* by Kalvin Schmidt-Rimpler Dinh
Nico, Rochereau, Roger & L'African Fiesta – *Volume 1 (1962–1963)* by Frank Gunderson

# 1964–1985 Affinità – Divergenze Fra Il Compagno Togliatti e Noi – Del Conseguimento Della Maggiore Età

Giacomo Bottà

Series Editor: Fabian Holt

BLOOMSBURY ACADEMIC
NEW YORK • LONDON • OXFORD • NEW DELHI • SYDNEY

BLOOMSBURY ACADEMIC
Bloomsbury Publishing Inc, 1359 Broadway, New York, NY, 10018, USA
Bloomsbury Publishing Plc, 50 Bedford Square, London, WC1B 3DP, UK
Bloomsbury Publishing Ireland, 29 Earlsfort Terrace, Dublin 2,
D02 AY28, Ireland

BLOOMSBURY, BLOOMSBURY ACADEMIC and the Diana logo are trademarks of
Bloomsbury Publishing Plc

First published in the United States of America 2026

Copyright © Giacomo Bottà, 2026

For legal purposes the Acknowledgements on pp. xi–xii constitute
an extension of this copyright page.

All rights reserved. No part of this publication may be: i) reproduced or transmitted in
any form, electronic or mechanical, including photocopying, recording or by means of
any information storage or retrieval system without prior permission in writing from the
publishers; or ii) used or reproduced in any way for the training, development or operation
of artificial intelligence (AI) technologies, including generative AI technologies. The rights
holders expressly reserve this publication from the text and data mining exception as per
Article 4(3) of the Digital Single Market Directive (EU) 2019/790.

Bloomsbury Publishing Inc does not have any control over, or responsibility for, any third-
party websites referred to or in this book. All internet addresses given in this book were
correct at the time of going to press. The author and publisher regret any inconvenience
caused if addresses have changed or sites have ceased to exist, but can accept no
responsibility for any such changes.

Library of Congress Cataloging-in-Publication Data
Names: Bottà, Giacomo, 1974- author
Title: Affinità–divergenze fra il compagno Togliatti e noi / Giacomo Bottà.
Description: [First edition]. | New York : Bloomsbury Academic, 2026. |
Series: 33 1/3 Europe | Includes bibliographical references and index. |
Summary: "Through analysis of the band's origins, the album as an artifact and its deeper
theoretical implications, the book explores CCCP's ambiguous position, their unique
sound and their lasting influence on European alternative music. The album's exploration
of cultural and national borders offers a unique rethinking of music and place in a time of
shifting geopolitical power dynamics, creating a distinct form of communication through
their music. Ultimately, this study reveals the band's out-of-time and out-of-place nature,
capturing their controversial yet pioneering role in shaping creative identities across
Europe"– Provided by publisher.
Identifiers: LCCN 2025025238 | ISBN 9798765111277 hardback | ISBN 9798765111260
paperback | ISBN 9798765111291 PDF | ISBN 9798765111284 ePub
Subjects: LCSH: CCCP Fedeli alla linea (Musical group) | CCCP Fedeli alla linea
(Musical group). Affinità–divergenze fra il compagno Togliatti e noi | Nationalism in music |
Punk rock music–Political aspects–Europe
Classification: LCC ML421.C423 B6 2026 | DDC 782.42166092/2–dc23/eng/20250603
LC record available at https://lccn.loc.gov/2025025238

ISBN: HB: 979-8-7651-1127-7
PB: 979-8-7651-1126-0
ePDF: 979-8-7651-1129-1
eBook: 979-8-7651-1128-4

Series: 33 1/3 Europe

Typeset by Integra Software Services Pvt. Ltd.
Printed and bound in the United States of America

For product safety related questions contact productsafety@bloomsbury.com.

To find out more about our authors and books visit www.bloomsbury.com and sign up for
our newsletters.

# Contents

List of Figures x
Acknowledgements xi
Timeline – From Band Formation to 'Affinità e Divergenze' xiii

**Introduction: There is a House in Fellegara** 1

1 **CCCP: A Band from Anywhere** 13

2 **Listening to and Looking at *Affinità e Divergenze*** 45

3 ***Emila Paranoica*: Imaginary and Affective Territorialization from an Italian Province** 75

**Conclusions: Post-Punk and Trans-European Cultural Sensibilities** 91

Bibliography 97
Index 107

# List of Figures

1.1 Places in West Berlin quoted in Zamboni (2017) and where CCCP played between 1982 and 1985. Image made on Google Maps  14
1.2 Giovanni runs in front of CCCP's gigantic red banner. Photo: © Umberto Negri and Shake Edizioni, from (Negri 2023c). Used with permission  33
2.1 Umberto, a collaborator of Superfluo, and Ignazio standing in front of the tape recorder and the Korg drum machine in the session for Ortodossia, May 1984. Foto © Umberto Negri and Shake Edizioni, from (Negri 2023c). Used with permission  47

# Acknowledgements

I wrote this book and take full responsibility for it, but there are several people I need to thank for making it possible. Fabian Holt welcomed me in the *33 1/3 Europe* series and offered editorial, methodological, and theoretical advice; Rachel Moore, Leah Babb-Rosenfeld, and James Eason smoothly took care of editorial work at Bloomsbury and Karthiga Sithanandam at Integra; Jacopo Tomatis shared with me some of the articles and scans from his archive; Luigi Ghezzi and Marco Benedettelli wandered with me around Kreuzberg to find the Willibald-Alexis-Straße during a rainy night of the *apocalisse*; the *Subcultures, Popular Music and Social Change* Facebook group offered collective wisdom as they usually do; Antti-Ville Villén listened to me complaining; Andrea Bottà helped with his infinite punk knowledge and private collection; my family supported me as always; Anita Degli Esposti of *Olga Dischi Volanti* made the interview with Fatur possible; Ignazio Orlando answered a Facebook message out of the blue; Guglielmo Bottin shared with me some of his expertise on drum machines; Bruno Dorella, Danilo Fatur, Emidio Clementi, Fabio De Luca, Helena Velena, Laura Carroli, Marcello Ganassini, Mirca Morselli, Sandro Sench Bianchi, and Umberto Negri answered my questions in interviews, private messages, and emails. I am grateful to Umberto for providing the pictures you find here.

I made all the translations into English, sometimes with the assistance of an automatic translator. The full responsibility for their faithfulness is mine; all lyrics of CCCP are originally in Italian, so are all the interviews I conducted. All lyrics have been checked from the official collection *Il Libretto Rozzo dei CCCP e CSI* ('The Rough Book of CCCP and CSI'; Ferretti and Zamboni 2022).

This book is dedicated to Berlin, a city that changed my life in less spectacular but equally significant ways as it changed the lives of the members of CCCP – Fedeli Alla Linea.

# Timeline – From Band Formation to 'Affinità e Divergenze'

Early 1980s – Massimo and Umberto rehearse together as Frigo, a post-punk duo/trio, and sometimes they use an old drum machine.

Summer 1981 – Massimo and Giovanni meet in Berlin and decide to start a band.

Early 1982 – Massimo, Giovanni, Pietro, and Zeo start MitropaNK; Pietro leaves the band; and they have first local gigs.

Summer 1982 – Umberto joins MitropaNK on bass; the band changes its name to CCCP – *Fedeli Alla Linea* ('Faithful to the Line'); and they play local gigs and some improvised shows in Berlin.

1982–1983 – The majority of the songs that will appear on the first three EPs and on the LP are written and rehearsed.

1983 – Zeo quits; the band acquires a first new drum machine; and first demo recordings and gigs around Emilia Romagna, Germany, and Holland as a trio.

May 1984 – The band holds a first session in Superfluo Studio (Bologna) and records songs that will appear on first two EPs.

1984 – Release of *ORTODOSSIA* ('Orthodoxy') EP; Fatur joins the band as dancer/performer; Annarella and Silvia join the band as dancers/performers; gigs around Italy, Germany, and in Barcelona; and the band acquires a new drum machine.

Winter 1984/1985 – The band holds recording sessions in Superfluo that appear on the last EP and on the LP.

1985 – Release of *ORTODOSSIA II* ('Orthodoxy II') EP ; release of *COMPAGNI, CITTADINI, FRATELLI, PARTIGIANI* ('Comrades, Citizens, Brothers, Partisans') EP ; gigs in Italy and Germany; and Silvia and Umberto leave the band.

1986 – Release of *1964–1985 AFFINITÀ – DIVERGENZE FRA IL COMPAGNO TOGLIATTI E NOI – DEL CONSEGUIMENTO DELLA MAGGIORE ETÀ* ('Affinity – Differences between Comrade Togliatti and Us – of the Achievement of the Age of Majority') LP

CCCP sign to Virgin Records and continue to release albums and play live until 1990.

2023–2024 – The band celebrates the 40th anniversary of *ORTODOSSIA* EP with *FELICITAZIONI!* ('Congratulations') Exhibition, followed by gigs in Reggio Emilia and Berlin and a summer tour around Italy.

# Introduction
# There is a House in Fellegara

It is late October 2023, and the warmest summer ever recorded until now extends its long tail into autumn. I travelled from Brussels to Reggio Emilia (hereafter simply Reggio)[1] to experience a museum exhibition and a reunion concert by the band CCCP – *Fedeli Alla Linea* ('Faithful to the Line'),[2] a band that shaped the Italian post-punk scene through an uncompromising attitude towards music making and live performance and through an original world-view, which was carried out from a provincial standpoint.

I first attended the exhibition that spanned the band's history and celebrated the fortieth anniversary of *Ortodossia* ('Orthodoxy'), CCCP's first EP from 1984. Later, I will have the utmost pleasure of attending the band's reunion and return to scenes in their Virgin Records (now Universal Music Group) quartet formation. This quartet featured Giovanni Lindo

---

[1] Pay attention to the fact that there is a second Reggio in Italy, Reggio Calabria, about 1100 km from Reggio Emilia. CCCP played there in the mid-1980s.

[2] The name of the band comes from the Cyrillic acronym for Союз Советских Социалистических Республик ('Union of Soviet Socialist Republics [USSR]') and is pronounced according to the Italian alphabet spelling as 'chee-chee-chee-pee'. Hereafter, I will only call them CCCP.

Ferretti, Massimo Zamboni, Annarella Giudici, and Danilo Fatur[3] with some guest musicians.

It is Saturday morning in Reggio, and I am cycling along a provincial road leaving the city behind me, with a clear goal in mind. The sun is shining, the air is clear, and still it is not too hot, making this a perfect day to be active. I rented what looks like a red children's bike in a shop close to Reggio's main railway station. Umberto Negri,[4] CCCP's bass player until the album under consideration here, and now a retired teacher/lawyer, sent me some directions because, according to him, location apps are of no use and lead to a dead end. I follow his message from my phone, which is precariously set in the bike basket, and cycle as fast as my tiny-sized single gear allows through what looks like an infinite plane of agricultural land. This is the lower part of *Pianura Padana*. Pianura Padana is a vast plane that takes up most of Northern Italy, is surrounded by the Alps to the North and the Apennine mountains to the south, is set by the Ligurian sea to the west and the Adriatic Sea to the east, with Milan at its centre, and is traversed from west to east by the river Po. It comprises thousands of acres of fields cut by dense urban conurbations, industrial estates, and mazes of motorway and fields. The latter are scattered by *cascine*, typical farmhouse settlements of red bricks that used to house small groups of peasant families.

Finally entering Scandiano, I find a sign to Fellegara, the sparse farmhouse settlement I am looking for. Along a narrow and asphalt road that cuts into straight angles following old property divisions, I pass some buildings which have been

---

[3] I will refer to them as Giovanni, Massimo, Annarella, and Fatur hereafter.

[4] Hereafter, Umberto.

renovated into middle-class residences, with electric fences and some daring design features. The pungent smell of pig manure fertilizer fills the air, and some farmers are busy tractor ploughing and pruning, with engines roaring. I pass the *agriturismo*, a kind of rural bed and breakfast that Umberto noted for me, and turn into a side road, where I immediately meet the carriage path leading to what used to be the rented home of singer Giovanni and CCCP's rehearsal space in their early years. This is the place where most of the songs contained in the LP *1964–1985 AFFINITÀ – DIVERGENZE FRA IL COMPAGNO TOGLIATTI E NOI – DEL CONSEGUIMENTO DELLA MAGGIORE ETÀ* ('1964-1985 Affinities – Divergences between Comrade Togliatti and Us – of the Achievement of the Age of Majority')[5] were written, took form, and were rehearsed (Contiero 2015). This is the headquarters of a band, a dream, and a story.

I get as close as I can to the farmhouse, walking the carriage path leading to it. It is clearly inhabited because voices can be heard and a few cars are parked outside. Are the owners the nearby pruning farmers? I don't dare ringing the doorbell on a Saturday morning, but I keep peering around, feeling like some kind of stalker. The house looks impotent with its three floors and the *porta morta* ('lobby' or 'entryway') to the side, and it is surrounded by tall, bushy trees and vineyards. When Giovanni discovered and rented it for cheap, more than forty years ago, there were only fields surrounding it. In the background, the gentle lines of the Apennines mountains provide some nuance to what probably looked like an infinite horizon of agricultural land – changing colours by the season, green in spring, yellowish in the summer, brown in autumn, and grey in

---

[5] Hereafter, *Affinità e Divergenze* as the band and fans refer to the album for brevity.

the winter – from the house upper floor windows, where the band rehearsed,.

This is CCCP's iconic equivalent to Kraftwerk's KlingKlang Studios and Andy Warhol's The Factory; however, it is not located in a dense urban setting such as Düsseldorf or Manhattan and is literally in the middle of nowhere. If we look for similar rural experiments, we can find them for instance in krautrock band Faust's rehearsing base in an old school of Wümme (Germany) or in The Stooges' Fun House (aka Stooge Manor) outside Ann Arbor, Michigan (USA). Like these urban and rural examples, the house of Fellegara became a place where rehearsing, living, planning, chatting, and creating happened in a free-form continuum. This included music making but also other artistic endeavours such as photography, painting, sculpture, and fashion, all conducted in do-it-yourself and experimental ways by a group of young men and women (Contiero 2015). CCCP members and hangers-on either lived in this house with Giovanni in semi-communal style or commuted nearly every day from Reggio and other surrounding towns by car, hitchhiked, or took some public transportation and then walked through the fields, passing railway tracks and small warehouses. I don't know if they dared cycle the twelve kilometres from Reggio, the way I did, because the provincial roads must have been much more trafficked than the present and drivers less cyclist friendly.

Yesterday, on a cheap coach bus from Milan to Reggio, I wrote down that the Pianura Padana, especially here close to the Bassa Padana, should be understood as *provincia diffusa* rather than *città diffusa*, that is, 'provincial sprawl' rather than 'urban sprawl'. It is far too wide open to maintain any urban feature. Its flatness makes past and present histories visible in unexpected ways: An old and tiny chapel façade melted into a bigger concrete warehouse wall tells how abruptly, violently, and recently industrialization took over these fields and how quick it also partially left. A mural on a lonely dry wall honours the *Partigiani Reggiani*, local communist partisans who resisted and eventually defeated fascism. The land is dry after an incredibly hot summer and seems to reject rainwater, while the air is among the most polluted in Europe; climate change is real.

But back to Fellegara in rural northern Italy: How to make sense of the sound of CCCP in a place like this? For many years I researched music in cities and experienced connections between the music and technologies of the modern city. In Düsseldorf, Germany, the *Autobahn* and railways looked like cables; every architectonical pattern a drum machine pattern; and every containership floating in the Rhine a synth loop. In Manchester, industrialization and deindustrialization had created a layered palimpsest as hard to read and angular as post-punk from there, but here in the Pianura Padana, what do I make out of these fields, this house, and especially this horrible smell? In my head I start replaying the track which closes *Affinità e Divergenze*, and I imagine the band rehearsing outdoors in the evening, sweating in the summer heat and pushing away mosquitoes, led by the simple drum pattern, *too-too-tah too-too-tah*, while they figure out the song's loose structure based on an E major riff on the go, something like a Patti Smith dirge slowly building up and filling itself with nightly images. The noise probably extended way into the fields, but the neighbouring houses were distant and vacant, probably just perceiving some kind of repetitive bass frequencies and the hypnotic chant of Giovanni growing into a scream of two words: *Emilia Paranoica* ('paranoid Emilia') as if he was furiously spelling them out to someone who didn't want to understand them.

Why on earth did CCCP end up in rural Fellegara? Were they simply hiding away from the 1970s' failure of radical political action or from the promises of the 1980s' new economic upswing based on consumerism? Was the self-exile into the middle of nowhere the only available strategy to be themselves or the only affordable one? Were these empty fields a sort of green screen for the projection of their dreams, fears, desires, and fantasies? What were these about? *Affinità e Divergenze* might be the answer to all these questions. It is their debut LP, released by the bolognaise independent label Attack Punk Records at the beginning of 1986, after three EPs titled *Ortodossia* (1984), *Ortodossia II* (1985), and *Compagni, Cittadini, Fratelli, Partigiani* ('Comrades, Citizens, Brothers, Partisans', 1985). It was subsequently re-released by Virgin Records in 1987, and CCCP became the first band to get signed by a major label in the Italian alternative scene.

The band was born four years before, in 1982, after the fortuitous and highly mythicized meeting of Giovanni (voice) and Massimo (guitar) in a Berlin discotheque in 1981. CCCP's stark image and multimedia performances combined Soviet and Eastern bloc aesthetics, Italian national popular culture, Berlin punk, local *liscio*, Asian music, commercial TV advertisements, new-wave, and avant-garde theatre in do-it-yourself and sometimes overtly provocative fashion.

*Affinità e Divergenze* was recorded in Bologna in the winter of 1984–1985 in Superfluo, a basic recording studio usually working with demos, commercials, radio jingles, and dance music. CCCP's set up was minimal with guitar, bass, and drum machine, overlaid with some artisanal sound effects. Giovanni's singing dominates the album with declaiming voice and idiosyncratic lyrics targeting the Eastern Bloc, mental health, consumerism, and existential issues.

The legacy of this album has rarely spread outside Italy, and CCCP's confrontational approach has always been interpreted purely within the Italian cultural landscape, thanks to their tongue-in-cheek attachment to the Italian Communist Party, to the Soviet imaginary, to their own little homeland Emilia, and to their mocking and meta-attitude towards the 'real' punks who called CCCP as sell-out posers.

# Outline and Some Explanations

In this book, I argue that the band's aesthetic, musical, and ideological approach in *Affinità e Divergenze* should be understood as an 'imaginary and affective territorialization' torn between maximalism and minimalism. I set my focus on the album's fascinating journeys across national and cultural borders. I argue that the album represents an unconventional but completely meaningful rethinking of music and place at the time. In the 1980s, cultural imperialism and geopolitical power balances were major topics of conversation in Europe. To unpack this intriguing situation, the book draws Doreen Massey's theory of space and Svetlana Boym's theory of the off-modern. I use these theories to discuss province, *Ostalgie*, and maximalism as elements apt in making sense of this album.

*Affinità e Divergenze* expresses the band's imaginary and affective territorialization first and foremost in their attempt to mix and shake musical, cultural, and geographical references in a free, amateurish, but programmatic way. Moreover, it shows in their relationship with high culture and literature. Both Giovanni and Massimo, the band's core duo, are 'provincial intellectuals' – as you might have found them in Carlisle, Antwerp, and Reims – people who found a way to escape the limits of class and of provinciality thanks to paperback novels and political essays, import LPs, film clubs, and backpacking. I argue here that what has been labelled 'post-punk' (Reynolds 2006) is the medium to spread basic communication, pleasure, and fun but also politics and art among a growing network of provincial towns and marginal centres across the Old Continent.

My analysis is based around critical qualitative methods, aiming on one hand at working with sounds, images, and lyrics, and on the other, at building a territorial understanding of music, where sounds always happen somewhere and where locality is in a complex and multifaceted relation with cultural production.

Primarily based on media 'texts', my analysis also draws from interviews and participant observation in and around Reggio and Berlin. My attempt is therefore partly hermeneutic, in reference to the album itself, and partly connected to an ethnographic stance, which looks critically at the relation between music and place.

I carried out interviews with former and current band members, people close to the band and to fans, but Massimo, Annarella and, I think, Giovanni decided not to interact with me. Their voices are missing and missed in this book, but I had to accept their silence. CCCP are band created out of stubbornness and determination, things that can crush you and the ones around you. Massimo and Giovanni have spoken widely about their work, and I therefore rely here on past interviews, book launches, events, talk shows, and gigs that are widely available online on platforms such as YouTube and on various on and offline media, duly listed in the bibliography.

Annarella's effortless work onstage speak for itself (Giudici, Ferretti, and Tagliati 2014). If in doubt, I cross-checked the authenticity of the online material I use in this book by contacting the people who uploaded it, by comparing on- and offline sources and examining non-digital archived material.

If you really think about it, when they signed a contract with Virgin Records, the band basically consisted of a singer, a guitar player, a drum machine, and two live performers (the bass player left the band at that point), and all this was happening in Italy, where the music ecosystem was dominated by dance music, *cantautori* ('singer-songwriters'), and *musica leggera* ('light music'; Tomatis 2021).

In the same era, in other European countries, bands born out of the same primordial soup of post-punk either started a long journey towards establishing themselves within global art niches, such as Einstürzende Neubauten or Laibach; dismantled and went into oblivion, except in some rare cases being rediscovered in some reissue and compilation; or went mainstream in their own national turfs, such as, to name a few, Die Toten Hosen in Germany, Indochine in France, Električni Orgazam in Yugoslavia and later Serbia, and Arno in Belgium.

Italy was somehow at the margins of this, and it was only in the 1990s and for a short time, that alternative music rose to the forefront, thanks especially to Dischi del Mulo and later Consorzio Produttori Indipendenti, record labels put up, not surprisingly, by Giovanni and Massimo, in connection to their new band Consorzio Suonatori Indipendenti (C.S.I.). These labels scouted, promoted, and produced a series of new bands including Marlene Kuntz, Üstmamó, and Wolfango, who were often recording in premises set up by the former CCCP themselves.

In one of their earliest unreleased songs, 'Oi Oi Oi', CCCP sang about being out of sync with time – too early or too late, and ultimately belonging to a different time than others. Their existence will always be a controversial matter, embedded in their out-of-time and out-of-placeness.

This book is divided into four chapters. Following this Introduction, the first chapter explores three perspectives on the origin of the band from the geographic locations of Berlin, Reggio Emilia, and Bologna. CCCP shows that where a band is from is a complex matter; it reflects spatial imaginaries and power-relations and shapes identities and self-perceptions, embedding sounds deeply into certain terroirs.

The second chapter is based on a close reading, observing, and listening of the album. I recently acquired a new re-pressed LP version of this album[6] that I use to analyse it as an artefact (cover art, insert, label, vinyl) and confront it with the other versions available on Discogs website. Moreover, I am going to pay attention to the sounds coming out of it and provide in-depth examination of all its songs. I tried as much as possible to explain this album to people who don't necessarily read Italian, you can definitely enjoy listening to CCCP without understanding the lyrics.

The third chapter, *Emila Paranoica*: imaginary and affective territorialization from an Italian province, brings in a theoretical interpretation of the album entering dialogue with thoughts about territorialization, affect, spatial imaginaries, maximalism and minimalism, and the off-modern.

In 'Conclusions: Post-Punk and Trans-European Creative Identities', I wrap up my main arguments and also report

---

[6] Universal Music Group – 0602458405217.

ideas from other listeners I interviewed, among musicians and scenesters that, for one reason or another, love or hate the band.

CCCP were ambiguous about their name and origin, vague in their adhesion to punk, and loyal in their attachment to the Soviet Union; this is confusing enough, but what does it sound like?

# 1 CCCP: A Band from Anywhere

The story of CCCP is not based on one specific subculture, local scene, or a particular music ecosystem; there is more than one city involved in their formation and development. This chapter illustrates the places and scenes which frame the band's formation and some of its stylistic and ideological choices. CCCP belong and make sense only as a band from Berlin as it is from Reggio and Bologna, as a band which is from a very specific but also very elusive anywhere.

## Ost-Berlin / West-Berlin / Trans Europa Express

*Berlin and the Long Twentieth Century*

CCCP are a band from West Berlin, where Giovanni and Massimo met for the first time in summer 1981. Unknown to each other, they had joined the mass of young backpackers who wanted to be remembered as standing by the Wall, to paraphrase Bowie, or, less prosaically, wanted to feel free in the most unpredictable place in Europe. Why did young people in the early 1980s want to visit a decaying portion of a city surrounded by a concrete wall and hostile forces? What does this have to do with music and with CCCP?

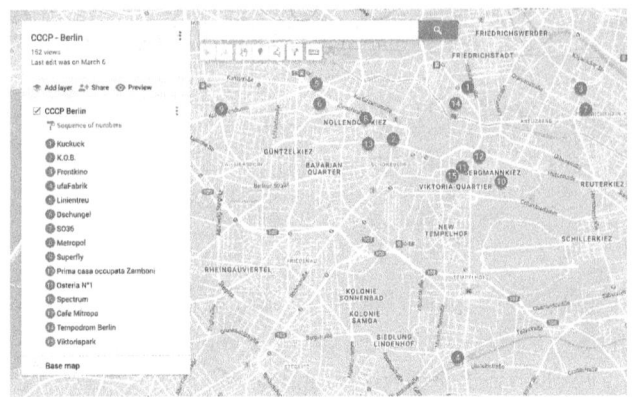

**Figure 1.1** *Places in West Berlin quoted in Zamboni (2017) and where CCCP played between 1982 and 1985. Image made on Google Maps.*

First, Berlin plays a unique role in European culture. In the aftermath of the First World War, in the roaring twenties as the capital of the Weimar Republic, the city became a site for avant-garde art and nightlife, gender roles were put into question, and expressionism gave way to new understandings of what cinema and theatre could do. It is in Berlin that the cultural industries as we know them today were first conceived and organized and where eccentricity became the norm. At the same time, it was a city where political confrontations between Left and Right, exacerbated by 1929 economic crisis, transformed streets into sites for radical protest and violence (Richie 1998).

The film *Kuhle Wampe, oder: Wem gehört die Welt?* ('Kuhle Wampe, or: Who Owns the World', 1932) exemplifies a lot of the aforementioned idiosyncrasies. The film thematizes unemployment, hunger, the power of the media, and political unrest from a collective left-leaning point of view, visible both on screen and in its production. A significant part of the film shows a left-wing sporting event for workers, where we witness the agitprop band Das Rote Sprachrohr (the red mouthpiece) taking the stage after male and female athletes all have been collectively and equally applauded. The band provides a performance which sits between theatre, dance, and music. Their scene starts with three women with mouthpieces reciting political slogans to the accompaniment of cheap and portable instruments, like banjos and accordions. All musicians wear the same sombre black minimal clothes; they walk around, whistle, exchange roles and positions in stern, austere, proto-militaristic ways. They move freely from performing music to staging a farcical political debate, and the scene ends with the 'Solidaritätslied' ('Solidarity song', written by Bertold Brecht for the film), in which they are joined by the whole crowd. The audience surrounds the stage on all sides, and the band choreographs its performance in an animated way. The same was probably happening during street demonstrations, where agitprop art was at the same time educational, multimedia, entertaining, and political. Some of these elements carry a not so surprising similarity to what was happening on stage at a CCCP gig, as we will see later. It is important to note that I am not building a direct lineage from agitprop to CCCP; however, it is important to note that certain kinds of avant-garde and off-modern cultural practices, born in the beginning of the twentieth century, worked as a living heritage, which in one way or another was transmitted down to punk and post-punk in non-linear and random ways, especially but not exclusively in Berlin.

Berlin fascinates also because it is the city of evil, where National Socialism was able to rise to power in the complex socio-economic situation and where the Holocaust was carefully planned and acted out. The city's eventual destruction and occupation during 1944–1945 sealed the end of one of the darkest eras that Europe had ever experienced. The material and psychological debris of this siege stayed with the city for a long time after the end of the Second World War. In my first visit in July 1989, I still vividly remember seeing bombed-out and burned buildings and shelled walls in East Berlin. This sinister, violent, and disturbed dimension still act today as a signifier for Berlin and Germany. Bands such as Joy Division, among others, dig into this middle European imaginary as a way to articulate both their desire to stand out from their boring English every day and a way to express existential fears (Bottà 2018). Moreover, sadomasochist and fetish scenes adopted and corroborated what has been referred to as 'Nazi chic' and 'Nazi thrash' (Stiglegger 2011). These days the use of harnesses, military gear of dubious cut, and leather are wildly popular among Berlin's techno tourists. CCCP's use of military stances and uniforms is of Communist origin, but often their connotations are confusing; moreover, the wild onstage antics of Annarella and Fatur also shift between the sublime and the perverse, sometimes influenced by the aforementioned trends.

Lastly, from 1945 to 1989, Berlin was an occupied and divided city, from 1961 with a wall encircling and materially sealing out its western part from the eastern side, following Europe post-Second World War geopolitical division into two opposing blocs. When CCCP visited the city, West Berlin was in an ambiguous legislative status, between being a *Bundesland*, a regional state belonging to the Federal Republic, and a city-state under the Western Allies control. East Berlin became the capital of the German Democratic Republic in 1949. The divided city mirrored Germany's partition into two states (the *Bundesrepublik Deutschland* (BRD) ('German Federal Republic') and the *Deutsche Demokratische Republik* (DDR) ('German Democratic Republic'), following a wider division between a capitalist Western Bloc, led by the United States and a socialist Eastern Bloc, led by the Soviet Union. West Berlin was a highly secured Western enclave in the Eastern Bloc and, therefore, gained a significant special status thanks to the *Berlinförderungsgesetz* ('Berlin subsidy law') that included tax subsidies and incentives. Moreover, West Berlin residents were exempted from BRD's compulsory military service for males. This brought many left-leaning young men who refused militarism to move to West Berlin. However, the city's working age population continued to shrink throughout the Wall years; portions of its housing blocks became vacant and, therefore, widely available, especially in the areas close to the Wall, to be cheaply rented and squatted in for living and creative purposes.

## *Neue Deutsche Welle*

From the late 1960s onwards, West Berlin became a West German and later European centre for radical political action, creative underground work, and fun, partly layered on its historical palimpsests as centre of the roaring twenties, as Nazi capital of evil, and as city of rubbles. The island city also became central in popular culture; films as disparate as *Cabaret* (1972), *Christiane F.* (1981), and *Wings of Desire* (1987) portrayed West Berlin as a past and contemporary hotspot for addiction, erotism, entertainment, and dream and helped revive a Berlin myth. Lou Reed published a *Berlin* album in 1973; David Bowie put up main residence there in the years 1976–1979, recording *Low* and *'Heroes'*, both 1977, and *Lodger* (1979); the Sex Pistols sang about the Wall in 'Holidays in the Sun' (1977); and Nick

Cave lived there for a while after his band Birthday Party split ('The Real Reason Nick Cave Moved to Berlin' 2021).

From the late 1960s, Berlin was also an interesting hotspot for German alternative music, first with *kosmische Musik* ('cosmic music')/Krautrock, thanks to acts such as Tangerine Dream and Klaus Schulze, free jazz with the Global Unity Orchestra, and left-leaning rock with Ton Steine Scherben.

Following the arrival of punk, young new bands started using German and experimenting with new harsh sounds. This scene was later canonized with the name *Neue Deutsche Welle* (NDW; 'new German Wave'). Among NDW's main features, musicologist Hornberger (2011) signals childishness, amateurish, and do-it-yourself attitude, the avoidance of Anglo-American influences, and the strong role played by isolated artists from the provinces and villages of the Federal Republic. Journalist Teipel (2001) in his oral history underlines the debt to North American and British punk, especially in the Hamburg and Berlin scenes, whereas author Esch (2016) emphasizes the idiosyncratic use of cheap synths and drum machines in creating a new uncompromising sound, especially in Düsseldorf. Lately, historian Lonkin (2024) has provided a wider take on this subject by referring to the fast step that the genre took from subversion to commercialization. She also expands its significance to other German-speaking countries (such as the DDR) and identifies issues related to gender and race. These latter arose also in connection to the attempt to blend international trends and German sometime antiquated elements. Historian Völker (2023) has developed a different approach to German music of the late 1970s–early 1980s, coining the term *Kälte-Pop* ('cold-pop'). In his view, coldness works as a programmatic metaphor and discourse, which is carried out in texts, sounds, and in the appearance of several acts, starting with Kraftwerk. However, the author notes a connection with aesthetic and cultural tendencies from the 1920s, to be found in the work of the aforementioned Brecht but also in Ernst Jünger, George Grosz, and Otto Dix. Cold-pop took an uncompromising turn in Berlin, where artists gathered into the *Geniale Dilletanten* ('brilliant *dillettantes*') scene used it to handle metaphors of war, downfall, and decay at a societal level and illness at an individual one. For instance, Einstürzende Neubauten and their singer Blixa Bargeld, in particular, continued to handle coldness and warmth as in a feverish delirium, both on stage and in their recordings.

## *Zwei kleine Italiener*

Several Italian artists addressed Berlin in their music in the early 1980s, ranging from Garbo with 'A Berlino va bene' (1981) to Franco Battiato with 'Alexanderplatz' (sang by Milva in 1982); however, in both cases, the city was a cold, ephemeral, and distant place, a metaphor for the Cold War atmosphere that the world was experienceing. It took two backpackers from Reggio Emilia to adjust the shot. Future CCCP's Massimo arrived in Berlin in summer 1981, guided by an article that appeared in the underground Italian magazine *Frigidaire* (Campo, Ferretti, & Zamboni 2005). He was at the time a student of Foreign Languages and Literatures at the University of Bologna, after a brief stint with Medicine in Modena. This journey and the following stay in Berlin have been the subject of *Nessuna Voce Dentro. Un'Estate a Berlino Ovest* ('No Voice Inside. A Summer in West Berlin'), a fictionalized memoir of that trip (Zamboni 2017), a theatre play, with the title *Nessuna Voce Dentro, Berlino Millenovecentottantuno* ('No Voice Inside, Berlin Nineteen Eighty-One', directed by Mariano Dammacco (2017), and a solo album of mostly cover songs from the Berlin days, called *Sonata a Kreuzberg* ('Sonata in Kreuzberg'), with Angela Baraldi and Cristiano Roversi (2018).

According to the book, after finding a room in a squat and a job in an Italian pizzeria, Massimo learned to navigate West Berlin's streets and their history, enjoying the freedom that the city allowed and reflecting on the geopolitical and historical controversies that surrounded it. He spent most of his time in Kreuzberg and Schöneberg (see Figure 1.1), districts that after the Second World War, due to their proximity to the Wall, were dilapidated and occupied in leopard-skin ways by the Hausbesetzerszene ('the squatter scene') that took over and often renovated empty and derelict housing complexes. Often sprayed with graffiti and murals and with banners hanging from windows, these houses were collectively run and offered an alternative to bourgeoisie family life through communal living for young, mostly white, Germans. Italian and more significantly Turkish 'guest' immigrants were also settling in the same districts, catering to the formers in terms of food and services.

Massimo also discovered German punk and NDW, thanks to the radio, to tapes and LPs of bands such as Felhfarben and Abwärts, and at live gigs. West Berlin had a wild topography of clubs and discos, ranging from experimental hotspots to commercially inclined dance floors. In places such as Spectrum, Dschungel, and SO36, Massimo learned the liberating effects of dancing and the celebratory and social role that this played in Berlin clubs, which is the primordial soup that will later transform the city into a celebrated techno capital. Each club, cellar, squat, bar, and discotheque had its own atmosphere and not only the mainstream clientele were dancing but also squatters. U.S. Army soldiers stationed in the city, artists, heroin addicts, politicians, and tourists were often mixing on improbable dance floors. In his memoir, Massimo explains how he pondered where to go dancing, describing SO36 as a place that requires 'too much brain, among those punk luminaries', *Spectrum* as crowded by 'too many *Besetzers*', *Dschungel* as a place where he could not go 'too ragged' and 'smelly of grilled food and pepperoni pizza', and *Superfly* as a 'leftover disco… positioned between rock and punk that loves to get stoned while waiting for a decision' (Zamboni 2017, loc. 99).

During the same summer of 1981, Giovanni, psychiatric operator, and radicalized drama, art, and music studies (DAMS) student at the University of Bologna on leave, reached Berlin by car, camping on a local lake with two friends who abandoned him to go to Prague. He was then hosted by some Italian acquaintance from his radical political days, where he also met Patti Vasirani and Spillo (sometimes named Pillo), two girls from Reggio (Campo, Ferretti, & Zamboni 2005). Giovanni was not particularly impressed by the *Frontstadt* ('frontline city') and was eager to leave the city for North Africa. However, on his last night, while at Superfly, a discotheque in Adenauerplatz, common friend Patti Vasirani recognized Massimo, dancing on his own to 'Alabama Song' in the middle of the dance floor, and introduced him to a feverish Giovanni.

Giovanni and Massimo, both normally residing in Reggio, had never met before, despite having common friends and frequenting the same scenes; age difference and profession might have played a role in their not knowing each other. This meeting sparked a long-lasting friendship and collaboration and set the basis of *Affinità e Divergenze* and several other albums, gigs, and projects in creative careers that today span more than forty years. In the following days, they used Massimo's accommodation in the squat as their headquarters and explored Berlin together, with trips to Hamburg and Amsterdam as well. Moreover, they started rambling about some creative collaboration, maybe a band, an idea that Ferretti had vaguely drafted for his master thesis project in ethnomusicology.

In Campo, Ferretti, and Zamboni (2005), Ferretti refers to a common visit to *Die große Untergangs-Show – Festival Genialer Dilletanten* ('The Great Doomsday Show – Festival of Brilliant *Dillettantes*'), that took place on 4 September 1981 at the Tempodrome. The festival celebrated the existence of a lively and creative scene in Berlin, which was making music in its own radical terms. 'Geniale Dilletanten' ('brilliant *dillettantes*'; with a naive spelling mistake in *Dilettanten*, the word for *dilettantes*) worked like a manifesto, linking an extreme brainiac attitude to child-like, amateurish, and do-it-yourself practices ('"Geniale Dilletanten". Subkultur der 1980er-Jahre in Deutschland', n.d.). Bands as diverse as Einstürzende Neubauten, Din A Testbild, and die Tödliche Doris, among others, future techno DJs, such as Westbam and Dr. Motte, and media celebrity Christiane F. took the stage under various monikers to perform a mix of music, noise, cabaret, performance art, and theatre in hysterical ways to an audience of 1400. Moreover, they all used German, defying the idea that popular music works only in English. They were also practising what Völker (2023) calls cold-pop. In one way or another, Giovanni and Massimo were taking notes. As Massimo writes in his memoir, German bands are cold and they transmit this to you. They infect with shivers… they are cold blooded bodies'. He describes dancing to DAF's 'Sato-Sato' as a way to warm up: 'we dance a military step, Sàto-Satò, marked, cadenced to the degrees, which does not demand sex, made of joints and sharp movements. Cold' (Zamboni 2017, loc. 100).

According to Giovanni (Campo, Ferretti, & Zamboni 2005), the two new friends took a one-day visa to East Berlin, where they were able to experience loyal-to-the-party-line socialism in its spectacular dimension, along the façades of Alexanderplatz and Unter den Linden. They shopped for communist patches and other memorabilia, probably in Zentrum. Back in the West, they also explored *Siemensstadt*, the nineteenth-century industrial conurbation of Spandau, and were fascinated by Berlin's Turkish presence and lifestyle in Kreuzberg.

## *MitropaNK*

These Berlin experiences, shared by hundreds of young tourists to the city in the summer of 1981, defined several of the steps that the duo took creatively back in Italy. Back to their precarious lives in Reggio, they started putting a band together, which was first complemented by Zeo Giudici on guitar and later drums and, for a short time, by a Pietro on drums. The band adopted a very Berlinesque monicker, MitropaNK, and started developing a few songs in Italian, focusing on Giovanni's psychiatric ward experience and elaborating some of the narratives and images they were confronted with in Berlin.

The name of the band is a programmatic portmanteau of 'Mitropa' and 'punk'. Mitropa, a contraction of *Mitteleuropa*, referred both to a scene café in Schöneberg, West Berlin, and to a GDR state-owned company responsible for restoration points on railways and motorways, that both Massimo and Giovanni visited in their trip along the crossing border motorways. Please don't be surprised by the duality in the origin of the name. This is as CCCP as it can get, and it is a strategy they continuously applied; everything in their world has always at least two meanings and attached narratives. Giovanni, for instance, likes to refer to the fact that Mitropa restaurants were the only places where East and West Germans, punks and politburo bureaucrats, sat and ate side by side, hinting at the pastiche between east and west that his band was aiming at.

MitropaNK were already a sort of meta-punk band, a punk band which from early on were reflecting on and restructuring what it meant to be punk and how to distinguish themselves programmatically from the North American and British models – a thing that CCCP perfected throughout their career but which was already there, as we will see later on, in early tracks, such as 'Valium Tavor Serenase', and which was deeply influenced by the attitude of the bands they saw live in Berlin.

According to Kromhout and Nieuwenhuis (2024)

> A widely shared feeling among the West-Berlin artists was that Germany, as an exponent of Western culture, had failed and was irrevocably broken.
>
> (p. 26)

Therefore, the geniale Dilletanten bands were using their native language because:

> After everything associated with Germanness had been contaminated by the Second World War, here was a chance to begin anew…. The do-it-yourself attitude and repurposing of the German language by the punk movement served as an act of self-empowerment. Geniale Dilletanten were members of a younger generation that tried to shape their own history.
>
> (p. 22)

This makes even more poignant the choice of MitropaNK to develop a music style which was punk-inspired but contained, from early on, elements of regional Emilian music and was sung in Italian. They were themselves experimenting with repurposing linguistic and cultural expressions using punk as an original and autonomous channel of expression.

In summer 1982, Umberto Negri joined the band on bass. He had previously rehearsed with Massimo in the short-lived project Frigo (note a first reference to coldness in the name, which means 'fridge' and might be inspired by the already mentioned *Frigidaire* magazine) and had some useful technician skills. As a quartet, after some more songwriting and rehearsals, they left again for West Berlin, with some friends and allegedly played some songs in improvised squat parties and were surprisingly well-received by locals. They also continued the aforementioned rhabdomancy explorations of the city. In a way, the band was testing themselves in Berlin, trying to figure out what the scale and the positioning of their success might become.

In his memoir as member of the band (Negri 2023c), Umberto refers to this Berlin summer as the one where they first considered CCCP as a possible new name. However, CCCP was already the name of an actual band from West Berlin, so to differentiate themselves they also added *Fedeli Alla Linea* ('faithful to the party line'), something Massimo picked up from a curious border controller but also the name of one of the clubs in Berlin they spent their time dancing (Linientreu), therefore providing another multifaceted explanation.

In winter 1983, the band has its most productive visit to Berlin, probably following an exploratory trip of Giovanni with Mirca Morselli, a friend with German skills and the president of Tuwat (more about that later). The trio, this time with a drum machine after the drummer's departure, didn't travel as backpackers with guitars but as a proper touring act, having secured gigs at Kukuk (25.11), Spectrum (26.11), K.O.B. (2.12) and allegedly appearing at the second edition of Atonal Festival in Pankehallen (4.12), followed by shows in Hamburg (Bar Centrale, 9.12) and Amsterdam (15.12 in Paradiso, same date as the Bollock Brothers[1] and 16.12 in De Verguide Koevet).

---

[1] It is possible that the Bollocks Brothers played on the main stage and CCCP in a lesser room. https://www.paradiso.nl/en/program/cccp-bollock-brothers/170085.

These dates appear on a flyer in the booklet of the rare EP published for *Stampa Alternativa* ('Alternative Printing') in 1990 and can be confirmed by several flyers and photos I consulted online. It is not possible to find confirmations about the band's Atonal participation in the festival programme; however, the festival poster contains a reference to a *Nebenbühne*, probably a smaller free stage, where the band might have performed.

Umberto remembers (…or not?) that:

> And then we had played at a festival, there was the *Atonal*, they gave us a side-stage and we did something. I seem to remember, I'm not very sure. But just like that, but really impromptu stuff.
>
> (Negri 2023a)

After a short German tour in 1984 that touched Stuttgart and Freiburg and did not reach Berlin, they were back in the city with the Wall for a last time in August 1985 for two dates, as a quintet, playing at UFA Fabrik. The concert on 28 August 1985 is available in its entirety on YouTube (Le Dinamiche 2023) and shows some of the tensions the band was going through and that would bring to the departure of Umberto soon after. Giovanni's ghastly expression is augmented by shaved eyebrows, bleached hair, and his skin looked unnaturally shiny and tight under the spotlights controlled by Mirca Morselli. He left the stage several times, sometimes to change costume. He moved thematically from Afghan robes to a Soviet uniform, from psychiatric ward pyjama to a punk overall. Both Massimo and Umberto had some technical difficulties and mostly statically ignored each other. It took a painful half of the show before the band clicked. However, both dancers and performing artists Fatur and Annarella worked effortlessly; they were a vortex onstage and continuously changed persona and look, chaotic but choreographed, in unison or alone. Once the full band entered the groove, a memorable performance ensued with gloomy performances of 'Noia' ('Boredom') and 'Allarme' ('Alarm'). The show ended with a long and troubled encore of 'Emilia Paranoica' ('paranoid Emilia'), which turned in the end into the Soviet national hymn; Annarella dressed as farmer and Fatur as industry worker stood on a makeshift pedestal, lifting their left fists as performing a socialist realist Soviet style monument, engulfed by white lights and feedback noises. The camera used for the video is static and shows only the stage surrounded by curtains, but a few people and shadows can be seen dancing frantically in front of the band towards the end, together with some brief sights of a gigantic CCCP banner hanging from the stage.

This is the last gig that the band would perform in Berlin until their reunion in 2023, when they played three sold-out shows at Astra Kulturhaus, under the label 'CCCP in DDDR', mostly in front of middle-aged fans that had flocked in from Italy.

# Emilia Mia, Emilia in Fiore

## *Reggio*

CCCP are a band from Reggio Emilia, a city in Emilia. Emilia is part of Emilia-Romagna, a hyphenated region of Italy that has given birth to an array of artists, some of them reaching international status, such as Zucchero Fornaciari and Luciano Pavarotti, or national status, such as Vasco Rossi and Ligabue. Genres such as liscio (more about it later) and Italo disco originate and still accompany dancing in the Adriatic coast of Romagna, the other half of this region. Emilia's towns like

Reggio, Carpi, and Modena are small provincial capitals with their own old and rich historical centres adorned by cathedrals, museums, opera theatres, and monuments. Until the late twentieth century and its demise, the Italian Communist Party (PCI) had ruled these city councils for decades, providing functioning welfare and well-being policies but also a stern and monolithic ideological leaning. Parallel to this political stability, local industry flourished, especially in the production of food (*Prosciutto di Parma* and *Parmigiano Reggiano* are from this area) and ceramic tiles, bringing a certain wealth, which is still today very much visible both in terms of infrastructures and in individual ostentation. This fascinating economic and political mix has been described as *Terza Italia* ('third Italy'; Bagnasco 1977), not fitting into the consolidated north–south dichotomy and blending socialist welfare with capitalist production in a way similar to Scandinavia, although only at the regional level.

Annarella and Giovanni were both born and partly raised on the Appennino, in rural villages sometime hard to reach even by car. Parallel to urban and industrial developments, Emilia is also a land of rurality and pre-modern traditions. The ritual *Maggio Drammatico* ('May drama') is an interesting expression of these traditions, consisting of a highly elaborated folk theatre in costume, taking place in open natural settings, with minimal decorations (Cavallo n.d.). It consists of amateur singers dramatizing mostly epics of medieval and Renaissance chivalry, with simple repetitive melodies of popular origin, with tragic, farcical, and sometime carnivalesque effects. *Il Maggio* is simple, do-it-yourself, melodic, and popular. The parallels with CCCP's live shows, which involved dancing, costume changes, and an overwhelming and sometime theatrical use of the voice, cannot be denied. Apart from the geographical origins, psychiatrist Benedetto Valdesalici, a charismatic figure that contributed to the early development and aesthetic choices of the band through pamphlets and graphics (Vinciullo 2015; Negri 2023c, 207), was a Maggio fan and expert. Giovanni himself as a former ethnomusicology student might have also leaned towards this tradition on his own.

## *Ahimé*

One of the first actions of MitropaNK was participating in the shooting of *AHIMÈ il congresso del mondo* ('Alas, the World Congress'), an experimental film by Claudio Oleari and, again, Benedetto Valdesalici (ubix 2012). In the film, Massimo, Giovanni and Zeo (Pietro had already been dismissed from the band) play a gig among disguised psychiatric patients and friends of the band. This is the final party, a sort of culmination of the movie, filmed in the Tiffany or Edelweiss discotheque of Castelnovo Monti.

The band brings a very Berlinesque atmosphere to the otherwise folk and psychedelic film, which focuses on absurdist scenes in the rural countryside of Villaminozzo, a small municipality in the province of Reggio. Over a few minutes, Emilia's scenesters and friends of the band, dressed as punks and goths but also as clowns and Russian soldiers, dance to the band's performing in a dark closed space, while other appearances watch. Both Annarella and Umberto, who were not yet in the band during the filming, are visible as guests. The stage décor includes a series of dancing Lenins, an icon that they used also in some gig posters (for instance for a gig at Mattatoio in Carpi on 19 September 1982). The score to the scene is not live, and edits rehearsal recordings from Fellegara consisting of several song fragments in their embryonal stage, some of which will be later recorded for *Affinità e Divergenze*, are included; for instance, Giovanni recites lyrics of 'Valium Tavor Serenase', and the band launches into a primordial version of 'Emilia Paranoica' and 'Sexy Soviet'.

What is clear in the few minutes of *AHIMÈ* featuring MitropaNK is their attempt to work out the Berlin influences in terms of the band's name, sound, ambience, and appearance and localize them into their own provincial and rural turf. Moreover, undeniable in the outfit of some of the hangers-on is the connection to the Maggio, at least in its carnivalesque visual dimension.

This film also determines the end of Giovanni's professional involvement with psychiatry. In the five years prior to forming the band, he had been a psychiatric operator, taking care of a group of mentally ill youngsters in an institution. This was happening in the middle of what can only be called a revolution in psychiatry that from Italy will later take over the whole world (Foot 2015). Since the early 1960s, psychiatrist Franco Basaglia had in fact started anti-psychiatric deinstitutionalization in Gorizia and Trieste, physically bringing down walls in mental institutions and devising alternative ways to take care of patients and to involve them in society. His work will be brought to the *Legge 180* (Italian Mental Health Act) in 1978, which formally abolished asylums.

According to historian John Foot (2015), this movement also interested Reggio Emilia, where psychiatrists Giovanni Jervis and Letizia Comba settled in 1969, after having contributed to Trieste's experience and started addressing mental health care in the total institution of San Lazzaro (the city's asylum) and shifting it towards an integrated systems of mental health centres active at local level. *Operatori* ('operators'), such as Giovanni, were recruited to work on the territory, with families and communities. The situation got increasingly difficult, because of the negotiations with the local Communist Party and ideological differences among psychiatrists, operators, and local institutions, which led to the conclusion of the most radical experiments in 1972. However, psychiatry in Reggio Emilia stayed at the forefront, especially in relation to this attention towards the territory; this experience was central to the legislative reform of 1978. The film *AHIMÈ il congresso del mondo* can therefore be also understood in terms of a creative activation of local mentally ill patients onto their own rural reality, as an alternative to asylum confinement. However, Giovanni's lyrics, as we will see, also reveal the complexity and human costs connected to this reform and the way mental health issues became more pervasive than normalized.

CCCP saw in Emilia a possibility to build a unique standpoint to look at the world, equally funded in local pride and in the attempt to expose the contradictions of the Terza Italia. From early on Giovanni said that the band could only have been born in Reggio Emilia, 'the most filo-soviet province of the American empire' (*Ortodossia* ['Orthodoxy'] EP booklet) and in live gigs he often announced 'Emilia Paranoica' with the words 'not in London! Not in Berlin! Not in New York! In Fiorano! In Sassuolo! In Scandiano!', for instance in a gig in Fiorano in summer 1983 partly available at Micheli (2011) or with variations of it as in Campo, Ferretti, and Zamboni (2005, 38–9). These words also appeared in the booklet to *Ortodossia* EP.

## *A Balcony in Santarcangelo di Romagna*

The first years of CCCP were very local. The band rehearsed in the aforementioned farmhouse, and most of their gigs took place in the Italian Recreative and Cultural Association (ARCI) clubs around Emilia-Romagna and in what I can only define as guerrilla gigs. For instance, during the May 1 celebrations in 1983, they played in various small towns on the Apennine mountains, moving on a hired truck that doubled as stage and apparently terrorized the unknowing inhabitants. These gigs were also the only ones with Mirca as substitute drummer, who will later become their light engineer.

In summer 1983 they performed in Piazza Ganganelli, the main square of Santarcangelo di Romagna, during the town's contemporary theatre festival, as seen on Terra Bomba (2014). Later, on the same day, they also played on a private apartment balcony, an event captured in probably the most iconic picture of the band in its early formation (visible for instance in the inner sleeve of *Ortodossia II*). A rumour even tells that Benito Mussolini, born in Emilia-Romagna, used the same balcony for a speech (Pustianaz 2012). On the first gig, the one the square which resurfaced on YouTube (Terra Bomba 2014), the band shows all its basic equipment made of one speaker, one guitar amp, a guitar, a bass, a drum machine, and a microphone. Their scenography however consisted of a gigantic red canvas with a stylized lighthouse and CCCP written under it (see Figure 1.2). The people circling the band seemed puzzled, Giovanni sang with his curved shoulders towards them, his hair a mess, the sound probably too loud, their attitude cold and confrontational, too confrontational maybe, even for a city where contemporary theatre was bringing all kinds of experimental shows and performances around. Moreover, they made mistakes. CCCP are not a tight hard-core band. Despite the martial beat of the drum machine, they were sloppy, and Giovanni often missed the beat; however, his vocal performance is strong, and Umberto's bass sort of anchored their sound back in place, while Massimo's guitar was restless and buzzy. It is the lyrics, however, which delivered a powerful and destabilizing message; they are a kind of lyrics that have

**Figure 1.2** *Giovanni runs in front of CCCP's gigantic red banner. Photo: © Umberto Negri and Shake Edizioni, from (Negri 2023c). Used with permission.*

never been heard before. Moreover, it was their appearance, some kind of Maoist-influenced proto-hipster look with high waist trousers revealing the ankles, sleeveless t-shirts, and canvas shoes which made them stand out from the provincial audience surrounding them.

## Punk and Province

The impact of the subcultural look in provincial towns and villages in the late 1970s and early 1980s was massive (Hornberger 2011; Pécout 2016; Goldhammer 2019; Worley 2020; Ballico 2021) and generated a moral panic which is incomparable to big cities, where extravagance is the norm, if not a means for survival. Punk invested the European provinces like a tsunami: The rules were easy and replicable; no awkward visit to an urban shop was needed; and you could find everything at home, preferably in a cardboard box of old clothes, ready for simple scissor cuts and primitive sewing. While it's essential to avoid relying on gender stereotypes, CCCP's sartorial interest was influenced by the stronger presence of female friends in this scene compared to others in Italy, which tended to be more male-dominated. One potential explanation could also be the members' age; unlike many other scenes, CCCP's members and friends were not teenagers but, rather, university students and workers, navigating varying degrees of personal and professional obligations.

Their local provincial status was also corroborated by an immense pride, although sometime tongue-in-cheek, in local achievements. Umberto for instance says that:

> the Reggio Emilians' idea is that the centre of the world is there. They think 'here is where the world's best food is'. They don't even know the towns in the neighbouring province of Parma. They don't care… 'What does it mean to be provincial? We have culture, we have cooperatives, we have an advanced model, we are not provincial at all'.
>
> (Negri 2023a)

Emilian towns are provincial but at the same time advanced, civic, and welfarist, creating opportunities for idle life and artistic endeavours. Moreover, as cities like Milan were banned from live touring due to riots and auto-reductions (Plastino 2023), many bands were redirected to Reggio Emilia:

> The Police arrived in Reggio Emilia in 1980, the Ramones came to play, Massimo had been in London, he had seen the Ramones, after a week they were in Reggio Emilia, we were there in the arena watching the Ramones.
>
> (Negri 2023a)

In 1982–1983, after a gig in Carpi, the band eventually discovered Tuwat, a punk hangout and cultural centre, with a name inspired by a Berlin squatter initiative meaning 'do something' in local German slang. Tuwat was a former public building where a small but active group of punks and activists squatted. Future CCCP dancer Danilo Fatur was active in Tuwat as handyman, barman, and sometimes performed a striptease-act under the moniker Josè Lopez Macho Frasquelo. In Tuwat, several Italian punk and hardcore bands performed such as Franti, Indigesti, Kina, and Contrazione among others.

Danilo says that:

> I was a bartender for this Tuwat collective, I did a little bit of everything cleaning etc and so it occurred to me that I wanted to do something artistic because the Tuwat was a kind of natural theatre, it was a club ok, it was like going into a theatre, there was the stage, the bar counter was made of shiny wire so for me I said I want to do something as an artist but it was… It was a pretty dark place, like being at the theatre more than anything else. There was a room where you could read the fanzines, buy a record, drink a tea and maybe even smoke a joint but let's say the entrance was pretty dark there was only the counter lit and clearly the concert room was always half-dark yes ok with the lights on the stage and the DJ booth and so and so it was. Apart from the fact that several foreign groups played there, it also felt like not being in Carpi, province of Modena, but I would say really in Berlin or anyway, maybe even in Spain, like in Barcelona yes. There was an international atmosphere, and I took the step, I started doing some male striptease to get out of my hibernation let's say, because I had just got out

after seventeen years in the boarding school run by priests, I wanted to let off steam.

(Fatur 2023)

It is thanks to this striptease show that Fatur got into the band and that was made possible in Tuwat, a place where the province was able to project itself and to perform an urban feel that was probably lacking outside its premises.

Emilia was, therefore, a space where CCCP were able to make space for themselves in performative sense, in ways which would have probably been impossible in a real metropolis. Their existence was suspended between provinciality and a cosmopolitan sense of belonging that the band would aesthetically and ethically never resolve. Especially for Giovanni, playing in villages of the Apennines was a way to maintain an identitarian attachment to the places and people that built his heritage, he wanted at the same time to take care of and to shock them.

Massimo, talking about his first return home from Berlin states that:

> We arrived in Reggio and somehow the world opened up to us. I suddenly felt that I really lived in Reggio. For the first time in my life, I didn't feel like a tourist here. We began to think that everything that was a defect could become a virtue, all we needed was to want it, it didn't even take a great intellectual effort. It was enough for Emilia to become the centre of our culture, of our way of seeing, and an enlarged Emilia also included Berlin, included the world of the East, included the Arab countries. But the centre was here. For us, Reggio had become the centre of the world at that moment.
>
> (Gasparini 1989)

## *The CCCP Logo*

It is in this period that their iconic stamp and logo started circulating. It is featured on the cover of *Ortodossia II* EP and on the side A label of *Affinità e Divergenze*. Inspired or, better, stolen from the *Order of the Red Banner of Labour* in its Type 2 version, the elaborate original badge involves a red star, hammer and sickle, a wreath, and a flag with CCCP written on it, all surrounded by a cogwheel inscribed by the words 'proletarian of the world unite'. It was a Soviet civil award assigned to honourable labourers. The band added 'fedeli alla linea' under CCCP and substituted the words in the cogwheel with 'punk filosovietico' ('pro-Soviet punk') on one side and 'musica melodica Emiliana' ('Emilian melodic music') on the other. Once again, we are confronted by a duality; the band is pro-Soviet punk but plays Emilian melodic music, and it is at the same time supernational and provincial, punk and melodic. In Italian, Emilian and melodic equal liscio (a term which is 'applied to four couple dances: waltz, polka, mazurka and tango' and which acquires fame all over Italy in the 1950s thanks to the Casadei family from Emilia-Romagna (Cámara de Landa 2002, 84). 'Musica melodica Emiliana' often appeared on posters of bands playing liscio in ballrooms. Liscio is today considered 'provincial, low-class and far too camp' and 'has a strongly local and working-class dimension' (Ghiglione 2022). This an overt provocation from the band; however, it also hides a programmatic attempt to provincialize punk into their own ecosystem, relying on singing in Italian and providing imaginary links via musical quotes, that I will show in the song analyses of 'Valium Tavor Serenase' and 'Allarme'. Emilia and the Soviet Union are the two main spatial poles of CCCP's imaginary and affective territorialization, while punk and 'musica melodica' are their sonic equivalents, both impossible and paradoxical in scope.

All living band members continue to live in Emilia-Romagna, apart from Umberto who lives in Turin.

# Skank Bloc Bologna

## *Attack Punk Records*

CCCP are a band from Bologna, the capital city of Emilia-Romagna, or at least Attack Punk Records, the independent record label that produced *Affinità e Divergenze*, was from there.

Attack Punk Records was founded by Giampaolo 'Jumpy' Giorgetti (now Helena Velena), Laura Carroli, and Carlo Chiapparini as an output for their hardcore punk band RAF Punk in 1981. They published a variety of EPs in a do-it-yourself and not-for-profit fashion, becoming a vanguard of the anarchist hardcore punk movement in Italy and building links to similar realities in the United Kingdom, Germany, Finland, and the United States. They discovered CCCP in 1983, and as Laura Carroli recalls:

> in Carpi, they were playing in this square, in this cloister, in short, they were playing in this environment, at the same time there was a concert that I've never been able to remember well, which was probably Raf[2] playing in the main square, so there was nobody there… Jumpy was always with his antennae on, and so we went to see this group that was playing, I wasn't impressed, I didn't give a damn, but Jumpy

---

[2] Italian pop star of the 1980s, known for the hit 'Self Control' (1984).

was immediately very impressed, so he went to talk to them and from there we stayed in touch, and then we asked them to make the record.

(Carroli 2024)

Helena Velena herself (at the time known as Jumpy) remembers that CCCP reminded her of the Dutch band Rondos that she had seen in a gig with Crass in the UK. However, she perceived CCCP's communism as a 'provocation, a sort of situationist boutade', which was also a bit provincial, whereas Rondos were close to a 'very serious workerist and Trotskyist discourse' (Velena 2024). Nonetheless, the label saw an opportunity in CCCP and decided to produce their first EP, which started selling more than the others and put the label under a lot of pressure to make a CCCP LP.

The three EPs and *Affinità e Divergenze* were recorded in Bologna. Giovanni had studied and lived there for some years, and Massimo and Umberto commuted there regularly to buy records, for gigs, and hang out. The city buzzed with creativity and its historical centre of porches, squares, and medieval towers was filled with students, *fricchettoni* ('freaks'),[3] and artists.

As already said, punk was the genre that the band programmatically decided to play – programmatically, because Giovanni and Massimo were slightly older than average snotty teenage punk rockers that were filling up garages in provincial Europe. Their music socialization happened in the 1970s, with progressive and blues bands. Giovanni talks about his approach to punk in an illuminating public interview given

---

[3] This is an Italian term adapted from the English *freak* that several of the interviewed used in reference to an early 1970s countercultural stance.

in occasion of the fiftieth anniversary of the opening of the DAMS study programme at the Università di Bologna (DAR – Dipartimento delle Arti 2021). In the mid-1970s as a radicalized student in the programme, he particularly enjoyed the study of ethnomusicology under the guidance of Roberto Leydi, the father of this discipline in Italian academia.

Giovanni refers to an unfinished experimental master's thesis project approved by Leydi, which would have consisted of exploring punk as 'the last avantgarde of the twentieth century' in the field, through participant observation, and maybe even creating a project band in a kind of practice-based thesis. This talk revealed his approach to creative work, his understanding of music in its visceral connection to culture as ways of life, and his ethnographic lens on places and sounds. Moreover, it shows how Bologna was at the forefront in contemporary understandings of popular music and its study.

## Bologna and the 1977 Movement

Bologna holds a unique place in history due to its political and cultural significance. Often referred to as Bologna *la Rossa* (Bologna the red), it stands as an example of Communist party administration thriving within a capitalist society. This nickname also reflects the city's long-standing left-wing traditions. Additionally, Bologna is known as *la Dotta* (the learned one), due to its prestigious claim as the home of the oldest university in the Western world. Thirdly, Bologna is also *la Grassa* ('the fat one') because of its connection with food. The city became a hub for intellectuals and creatives, especially within the creative wing of the *Movimento del 77*, a countercultural and diverse radical Left movement that rose during the 'long' 1970s (Gotor 2022).

The year 1977 was one of political turmoil in Bologna, culminating in the shocking murder of Francesco Lorusso, a student known to Giovanni, at the hands of a police officer during a demonstration. The following days and weeks were very tense with arguments among different factions about possible political reactions and a repressive state response, which also involved armoured vehicles patrolling the streets of the centre. The local Italian Communist Party had also been in an ideological dispute with the students, and the drift rose once Radio Alice, a local free radio close to the *Movimento*, was raided and closed. That year was a turning point for many in Bologna, including Giovanni, whose identity was split between his rural origins, loyalty to the Communist Party and Catholic faith, and his life as a bolognaise urban radical student and member of extra-parliamentary group Lotta Continua ('Continued Fight').

The dramatic turn of events in 1977 made many look elsewhere for whatever they were aiming for. Alternatives included going underground and joining armed terrorists; heroin addiction, which rose considerably in these years; travelling East and investing in non-violent action inspired by Buddhism and other forms of non-Western religions; and then punk came.

Sench, a fan of CCCP and musician in a coeval band from the Como Lake called Potage, with a similar Lotta Continua political background as Giovanni, told me that punk gave him the opportunity to be against people without having to convince them of anything:

> We were sick and tired of going and telling people... that they should think the same things that we think, the things that are right... let's go and tell them to fuck off while

> maintaining something of a root of imaginary approach of what we used to do
>
> (Bianchi 2024)

Also, Laura, a member of bolognaise punk band RAF Punk and of Attack Punk Records, shared this perspective and saw how in the Movimento:

> I had no real role there and was always intimidated by the very important personalities, by the leaders who seemed very distant…I felt very small very insignificant, yes that changed then with punk (Carroli 2024).

Punk sort of gave an alternative way to be creative and to change the system, removing politics from direct, violent and mass action, and translating it into do-it-yourself subcultural and affective work. This chaotic period, including the March riots, even inspired the UK post-punk band Scritti Politti to write the song 'Skank Bloc Bologna'.

## *Punk Bolognese*

Between 1977 and 1981, Bologna saw the emergence of a vibrant punk scene, with strong ties both to the local social movements and the broader Italian counterculture. The year 1980 was a turning point for the city's music and political landscape. The Clash performed in Bologna's main square, an event that symbolized the city's connection to the international punk scene. This same year also saw the formation of the Anarcho-punk network, further solidifying Bologna's role in the cultural revolution of the time. RAF Punk members contested The Clash gig and distributed a leaflet in which they accused the London band to be sell-outs (Bottà and Quercetti 2019). At the same time, post-punk and no-wave were also creating a very active, international, and arty scene in Bologna thanks to Gaznevada, Skiantos, Confusional Quartet, and the so-called Italian Records (Ottone 2021; Zuffanti 2021).

CCCP were aware of this cultural melting pot, available less than one hour away from their own headquarters. Umberto refers for instance to the fact that:

> in Bologna there were so many things, one of the things that was really a blast for me was this festival of No Wave, so it was called, there was James Chance and the Contortions, which was a real blowout.
>
> (Negri 2023a)

However, they refused to be absorbed into this cosmopolitan and urban dimension. If they wanted 'urban', they went to Berlin and always maintained an ambivalent and provincial relationship to Bologna.

Their recording sessions in town are remembered, for example, by Umberto for 'travelling back and forth by train and car from Reggio to Bologna. I remember every bend in the road as if it were yesterday' (Negri 2023c, 436). Massimo refers to the fact that the Superfluo Studio was underground, so were the canteen and the bar where they went to during pauses (Ob&k 2015b). Moreover, despite being produced by an anarcho-punk label, they always kept distance from the hardcore anarchist scene, with the only concession being playing a cover of 'Tube Disaster' by Flux of Pink Indians in their early days.

CCCP played in Bologna several times in their career. On 21 May 2024, the reunited band played in piazza Maggiore, the same location of the infamous 1980s' Clash gig. On the contrary to that gig, this one was not free, and the square was cordoned off, bringing a series of contestations, with Helena Velena, once again, on the forefront (Papa 2024).

# 2  Listening to and Looking at *Affinità e Divergenze*

*Affinità e Divergenze* is CCCP's first LP and, just like the previous three EPs, is recorded in Superfluo Studio in Bologna, with the band's minimal means and instrumentation, track-by-track, with each member playing their part separately. This chapter examines the album as an object that can be looked at, read, and played, but also describes the instrumentation that CCCP used in recordings and performances. Even if the musical instruments themselves have no agency if not played, programmed, and started, I believe that their role in the making of this album is as significant as the performers themselves and therefore need some attention, starting with the drum machine.

## The Machine Says *boing_boom_tschak*: CCCP and their Instrumentation

Zeo Giudici, the brother of Annarella, was the drummer of MitropaNK and early CCCP but left the band because of compulsory military service in 1983, leaving the drums duties vacant. Mirca Morselli, president of the association that ran

Tuwat in Carpi, covered for some guerrilla gigs in May, but attempts to find a new steady drummer were fruitless. The ad they used and that appears in Umberto's book (Negri 2023c, 237) tells of a band with 'high morality' looking for a drummer who is 'draft-exempt, grumpy and indefatigable' and asks 'rock drummers', among others, to abstain from contacting. No wonder why only a few random people answered.

Umberto and Massimo were already using a drum machine in their short-lived experiment Frigo, probably an old-fashioned Italian model from the 1960s, something like a Welson Super-Matic S12, a Farfisa Rhythm10, or a Elca Drummer 1. CCCP seems to use this old rhythm box in at least one song in the *Altro che Nuovo Nuovo* ('Nothing but New New') live album from 2023, recording of a gig in Reggio Emilia in 1983, but still with Zeo on drums in most songs. You can hear the steady pre-set rhythm without variations for instance on 'Sexy Soviet'.

Once they quit looking for a drummer, they opted for a new programmable one, a Korg KPR77 (visible on Figure 2.1), which forged the sound of CCCP's incarnation as a trio. It was an entry-market Japanese instrument with analogue sounds that could be programmed. The drum machine programming was taken very seriously by Umberto and Massimo, who spent days figuring out sequences and individual sounds – sometimes based on what Zeo had played but also expanding the possible rhythmic palette thanks to technology.

There are several bootlegs on YouTube (Terra Bomba 2014, 2022; Zarucchi 2021) dating from 1983, where the sound of this drum machine seems tiny and cheap, mostly providing basic and not too intricate arrangements to the linear

**Figure 2.1** Umberto, a collaborator of Superfluo, and Ignazio standing in front of the tape recorder and the Korg drum machine in the session for Ortodossia, May 1984. Foto © Umberto Negri and Shake Edizioni, from (Negri 2023c). Used with permission.

unfolding of the songs; moreover, it was the adequate object to comply with the band's stern aesthetics, turning CCCP into a truly displaced Berlin band. The lack of a drum kit, the main signifier of rock music, was frowned upon by audiences worldwide (LeRoy 2022) but was initially compensated by passing the drum machine signal into an old TV screen and by the gigantic red banner with the name of the band and the lighthouse.

However, in 1984, this first drum machine melted or broke down. According to Negri (2023b), the band went to the Merula Music Shop in Bra (Turin), famous in Northern Italy, to get a Yamaha RX5 or an RX11. In the CCCP exhibition in Reggio in 2023–2024, a RX5 is exhibited, but its production began in 1986, while a RX11 was available in 1984. Musicologist Bottin (2024) refers to a RX11. This is the instrument that allowed the band to develop, expand, and play live the songs of *Affinità e Divergenze*.

The sounds from the Yamaha are samples, and the machine has a memory function, expandable via c-cassettes. Umberto referred to the fact that 'the internal memory of these drum machines was not enough so we had to load another bank of memories onto cassette tapes. At some point we started playing these tapes with data on the PA before the gig' (Negri 2023b). This is something that also Mittagspause in Germany were doing (Bottà 2020, 105–6), but used data cassettes for electronic typing machines.

According to Orlando (2023), in studio these drum tracks were then passed and recomposed onto an Oberheim DMX, with some minimal variations. The DMX is a professional and sophisticated studio machine that you can hear, for instance, on New Order's 'Blue Monday' and a favourite in hip-hop productions (LeRoy 2022). It is not surprising that such an expensive machine was present in the Superfluo Studio, which was producing jingles and Italo disco hits. The drum sounds you hear on *Affinità e Divergenze* are, therefore, from this DMX.

Throughout his career with CCCP, Umberto used the same bass, a brown Cimar 2072 MH, that at a certain point he painted light blue and started modifying by sawing though the headstock and body. Cimar was a Japanese sub-brand of Ibanez, and this model was very similar to a Fender Jazz Bass. He bought in a music shop in Modena with Massimo, who on his part acquired what looks like a red Ibanez Blazer BL500 ('1982 Ibanez Blazer Series Catalogue' 1982) that he played live through a Marshall head and speaker cabinet and was not using any pedal effects, except for maybe a fuzz box. Both string instruments were affordable entry-level Japanese ones and were used on the recording of the album. In a few songs on the album, an acoustic guitar is used, but I received no indications about its origin because it was never played live. I also don't know what guitar amps were used in the recordings because several were probably available in the studio.

The band had also acquired over the years a bunch of simple and sometimes antiquated instruments that they creatively used: Umberto played a metallophone that had to sit live on a trestle, Massimo played a harmonica from his blues-rock teenage years, a melodica, and experimented with a soprano sax. In her brief time in the band as performer, Silvia Bonvicini[1] also played a Casiotone VL-1 live, but I cannot figure out if that has been used on the LP.

---

[1] Hereafter, Silvia.

## Superfluo

Throughout the first three EPs and *Affinità e Divergenze*, the band had basically the same set-up live and in studio. This instrumentation was made of cheap entry-level instruments and other 'found' or second hand musical objects. This was partly due to their do-it-yourself punk attitude and partly because of pure economic restraints. All effects on the recordings are therefore based on studio equipment and on the work of the sound engineer Ignazio Orlando and of the producer Carlo Chiapparini. They both later joined CCCP as 'hired guns' after the band signed with Virgin Records.

Ignazio was running Superfluo, a small studio, in a cellar in the centre of Bologna, close to a tram line. Laura Carroli of Attack Punk, remembers how they possibly chose it:

> Bologna is small, in short, the places are few, so there was this studio that was cheap, and Ignazio was there, and then later he went to play with them… I don't remember exactly who told us about it, but it was a decent studio, quite cheap, a good compromise… it was in via San Felice, it was a cellar on Via San Felice, and you were going down a staircase, and there were those little windows on the street that come out of cellars, so the noise also came out on the street, and on Via San Felice there was also *Italian Records*, practically at the same height, so it must have come out under those circumstances, also because Ignazio played in *Luti Chroma*, which was a band involved with *Italian Records*.
>
> (Carroli 2024)

In fact, Harpo's Bazaar, which developed into Italian Records, had already settled in Via San Felice 22 in 1977. The presence of Superfluo on the same street didn't come as a surprise; rather, it was a manifestation of some kind of creative clustering taking place in Bologna, a city where radical politics and creative work went hand in hand, as shown in Chapter 1.

The studio was used in two main bookings, the first in May 1984 for songs featured mostly on the first two EPs and the second in the winter 1984–1985 for what you can find on the third EP and on *Affinità e Divergenze*. Umberto notes (Negri 2023c, 382) that the studio initially had a Fostex eight-track reel-to-reel tape recorder (see Figure 2.1), and according to Helena, the studio was using ¼-inch tapes thanks to a new technique, that allowed you to:

> record up to eight tracks on this tape. The reels like that costed a lot less than the others, the ones used for mastering were exorbitantly expensive… it allowed us to make records, let's call them of semi-professional quality, now to give an idea which is realistic, credible enough. It was a fundamental thing.
>
> (Velena 2024)

Umberto talks about a sixteen-track reel-to-reel tape recorder used on *Affinità e Divergenze*, which implies an upgrade between the first and the second recording sessions (Negri 2023c, 416). In his description, the studio had an atrium with a reverb plate, a recording room with the mixer and the tape recorder, and a vocal booth behind a glass (Negri 2023c, 373).

Umberto referred to an artisanal reverb plate / spring reverb, that was widely used in the recordings, consisting of:

> this big wooden box on the floor with… there were bedsprings in it with two transducers or microphones, I don't know what, one on one side and one on the other, one went in with the sound and you could hear all the vibrating of the springs, they're those old bedframes, you know the ones with all the springs?
>
> (Negri 2023b)

## *Affinità e Divergenze* as Object

*Affinità e Divergenze* appears in twenty-three different versions on Discogs (*CCCP – Fedeli Alla Linea – 1964–1985 Affinità-Divergenze Fra Il Compagno Togliatti E Noi Del Conseguimento Della Maggiore Età* 1986). Attack Punk Records published two versions of the LP (plus a test pressing), the first in red vinyl and the second in dark red vinyl. Later versions, plus tapes and CDs, are re-issues by Virgin Records, EMI, and Universal. Virgin signed the band in 1986, acquiring its back catalogue from Attack Punk Records, but the entity of this step and the possible use of the master tapes in the major label pressings remain obscure (Zarucchi 2025).

The first LP record is pressed on red vinyl and is marked with the catalogue number 'Attack Ottobre/10' on both the side A label and the spine. October 10 is an important day in the Russian Revolution and might be referenced in this code. After a few copies were distributed, the label started adding a coloured insert. The insert came in various colour combinations, such as red text on green paper, blue text on yellow paper, and more. According to Discogs's notes, also a smaller white insert with identical red text but no image is known to exist. The insert has a short text written with an early computer or an electronic typewriter and signed 'Attack Punk Records / Multimedia Attacks' followed by an address and telephone number from Bologna. The text, titled 'many questions, and also an answer…' is a kind of statement, supposedly responding to some complains about the lack of a track list and other information on the album. A music journalist, Luca De Gennaro, is explicitly named and might be one of the dissatisfied, but the text sort of increases the mystery surrounding the band and their intentions, although it did provide the song order. Despite not authored, Helena Velena of Attack Punk noted that:

> there is a whole series of materials and things that I have written. And that if you go check them, you see that there is a different slant. You can find in them the deterritorialisation discourse, the situationist approach, you can see that it is completely different from their kind of rhetoric... The text of the famous green flyer that was reprinted recently, for example. I re-read it recently, I found exactly my own words and rhetoric in it... if you go and read it, you see that it tells about CCCP, the way I was seeing them.
>
> (Velena 2024)

Under the text there is a picture of Annarella in black robes, with open hands, probably a screenshot from a 1985 television special about the band for the show *Obladì Obladà* on RAI, the Italian national public broadcasting company.

The original inner sleeve is a white double-hole sleeve stamped with LFN 5/86. An additional A4-sized, 28-page booklet titled CATALOGO was sent to buyers through some mail order. The booklet contained the lyrics to all Attack Punk recorded tracks, typed on a type-machine and xeroxed, with some cut-out images, drawings, and graphics.

According to Discogs (*CCCP – Fedeli Alla Linea – 1964–1985 Affinità-Divergenze Fra Il Compagno Togliatti E Noi Del Conseguimento Della Maggiore Età* 1986), the run-out grooves of the original record have etchings: side A reads '*VICINI PER QUESTIONI DI CUORE...*' ('close because of matters of the heart...'), and Side B reads '*SE COSI SI PUO DIRE*' ('if one can say so'). The runout also bears the marking MPO, which likely indicates the pressing plant, but this etching is 'scrawled and difficult to read'.

The band conceived the cover of the LP with Carlo Chiapparini (aka Bounty Scarponacci, guitar player with RAF Punk, producer of the LP for Attack Punk Records, and graphic designer). Green is the dominant colour of the cover, which consists of a combination of texts and images. The top is dominated by two dates: 1964 and 1985, which are on both sides of a circular portrait of communist politician Palmiro Togliatti. Overexposed to the portrait are five torso cutouts of the band members: Annarella, Fatur, Giovanni, Massimo; and Umberto; these black-and-white images are, at sight, either photocopied or hand-sketched from photo shoots. Fatur, in the interview I had with him, pointed at himself on the cover and said that his picture had a political, although cryptic, connotation:

> I am this one with the deadbolt… more or less it means let's free the comrades from prison, I had stolen the deadbolt… I believed in these things, do you understand?
>
> (Fatur 2023)

Annarella has a diva pose with a cigarette in her hand and sports a headband; Giovanni looks straight ahead with a microphone in his hand, wearing a military half sleeve shirt; and both Massimo and Umberto look focused on their, not visible, instruments. Under them a gigantic red CCCP with white contours takes the whole middle part of the cover, followed underneath by a red FEDELI ALLA LINEA. Underneath in three lines of different sizes, the whole long and enigmatic title of the album in white. All letters are capital, in Roman style. The cover is therefore printed in three main colours: green, red, and white, which are also the colours of the Italian flag. The vinyl record itself was red in its first original pressings as was typical for the label.

The back cover shows Silvia, who had briefly been in the band, with a headband and in a fur coat, with a podium behind her reproducing the one in the front in a wider and oblique perspective, with Togliatti's portrait, the years, and the text, but the band members are missing. On a wall on the side of the building, there are the band's and the label's logos (which are also the record's paper labels) and a pseudo-Cyrillic 'Attack Punk Records', which disappears, together with the label's logo, in the Virgin copies issued from 1987 onwards (but reappearing in the 2024 *Felicitazioni!* ['Congratulations'] edition). On top of the podium, a pencil-sketched portion of a gigantic hammer and sickle is visible. The podium might be a reference to the guerrilla gig the band played on a balcony in Santarcangelo but also convey a martial totalitarian feel, which might be even misinterpreted, at first sight, as fascist.

The kilometric title of course tells a different story, engaging with communist politics at a variety of levels. The two dates 1964 and 1985 are respectively the dates of Palmiro Togliatti's death and the expected date of the album release (even if that, as seen, would happen in 1986). Togliatti had been one of the founders and, until his death, the secretary of the Italian Communist Party and a privileged Western interlocutor of the Soviet Union, where a city was named Тольятти Tolyatti in his honour. The LP title refers to divergences between comrade Togliatti and us, the title of an article first published on 31 December 1962 in the Chinese Communist Party newspaper *Renmin ribao* and translated into Italian in a booklet edited by the 'Casa Editrice in Lingue Estere Pechino' in the same year. The band stole the title and added *affinità* ('affinities') to the polemic Chinese stance. The band seems to say that we are having both affinities and divergences with Togliatti, we are in dialogue with him, we are his heirs, and we continue to be faithful to the party line, whatever it might be.

The rest of the title might come as a kind of subtitle because of a hyphen visible on the record label and on the spine (but not on the cover): *Del conseguimento della maggiore età* means 'on reaching the age of majority'. This could be a reference to the twenty-one years elapsing between 1964 and 1985. Until 1975, twenty-one was the legal age of majority in Italy, which for instance had interested Giovanni (born 1953). The twenty-one years between 1964 and 1985 represented a continuous distancing of the far Left from the Communist Party line and a dispersal into radical and sometime conflicting minority positionings, which, again, had involved Giovanni as a student in Bologna. Was this distancing going to end with the coming of age? Or is the coming of age the real final emancipation from Togliatti? Are CCCP the band that return to the 'adult' Soviet-led Communism? Or has *riflusso* won, and consumerism dictates the life of Togliatti's children these days?

Let's give the record a spin to find out.

## The Songs

*Side A*

'CCCP' is a kind of manifesto for the band and the perfect opening track for their first LP. The song starts with an angular but slow bass riff, some long harmonica sounds, and sinister noises which resemble someone loading a gun or tampering some deadbolt. The atmosphere has something of a Morricone film but is also definitely indebted to The Cure's 'Subway Song', which starts with the same kind of instrumentation and mood.

Umberto says that he came up with the bass riff in the late 1970s inspired by the no wave (Negri 2023b). Massimo plays harmonica, an instrument that he played since his blues-rock teenage years, but I am left unsure of who is taking care of the noises. Umberto told me that Fatur, who had recently joined the band, is responsible for that, as the band's main noise-maker, but Fatur himself does not remember (Fatur 2023). I will therefore leave this open.

After the sombre intro, Giovanni's voice screams 'CCCP' followed by a highly syncopated drum machine track and Massimo's *grattuggiare*,[2] while the bass riff continues. Giovanni re-enters after a while with convulsive cut-up lyrics involving commercial slogans followed by a list of Soviet bloc newspapers, repeating 'KGB', going back to a cut up of commercials and getting to the refrain where he sings '*fedeli alla linea*' three times followed with 'CCCP' and 'SSSR', that is, the Italian and Russian spelling of the band's name. The second verse refers again to faithfulness to the party line even if it doesn't exist and then introduces an emperor, who is sick and dubious. This image of a sick emperor reminds me of a Franz Kafka's short story, originally titled *'Eine kaiserliche Botschaft'* and in Italian, '*Un Messaggio dell'Imperatore*' ('A Message from the Emperor').

Both the short story and the song talk about faith in something which is not there and cannot be achieved for real. In Kafka, it is the architectonic and bureaucratic order

---

[2] It might have been Giovanni who started to refer to Massimo's frantic right-hand work on guitar as *grattuggiare* (to grate); for instance in Campo, Ferretti, and Zamboni (2005, 33), he tells of a 'grattuggia impazzita' (crazy grater). This verb is used in Italian mostly in reference to Parmigiano Reggiano, parmesan, which is an Emilian product, adding another local layer to the band's work.

which makes the messenger unable to deliver the emperor's message to the simple subject, leaving this one to dream about it. CCCP maintain the same impossible faith in the party line, despite being overflown by capitalist consumerism and by the promise of something new. In truth, the words *nuovo nuovo* (new new) could also be a tongue-in-cheek reference to the *Nuovi-nuovi*, which refers to an Italian art movement, deeply influenced by postmodernism. Renato Barilli, Francesca Alinovi, and Roberto Daolio launched this movement via an exhibition that they curated at GAM in Bologna in 1980 (Barilli 2006, 60). In 1984 Barilli and Daolio curated a Nuovi-nuovi exhibition titled '*Una generazione postmoderna. Iconici, aniconici, immagine elettronica*' (A postmodern generation. Iconic, aniconic, electronic image') in Reggio Emilia. Giovanni uses the expression *altro che*, which is difficult to translate. In case this is a fragment stolen from a conversation, as sometimes happens with his cut-up lyrics, it might mean something ironic like 'even better than…' or 'completely different than nuovo nuovo'. It states a defiance of postmodernism and an affirmation of the fully modern stance of the band.

The second verse introduces the drum machine used to its full potential with humanly impossible tom fills and handclaps reprised after the second refrain and faded out. The drum machine is not substituting a human drummer anymore, nor it is leading one to dance as in an Italo disco track. It is an all-pervading instrument which defines the unique sound of CCCP, take it or leave it.

'Curami' is the only song whose origin is not Fellegara or Reggio Emilia but Berlin. Massimo showed the guitar riff to Umberto in the cellar of Kunst- und Kulturzentrum Kreuzberg (KuKucK), a gigantic Berlin squat on the Anhalter Strasse 7, where the band lived and rehearsed between gigs in winter

1983 (Negri 2023c, 301). Listening to the riff, Giovanni said that it sounded like The Cure, a band that they were all fans of, and 'cure' soon turned into *Curami* (Ob&k 2015a).

The song starts with a muted descending guitar riff and with a simple metallophone melody (that will return in the end) played by Umberto, while the drum machine accentuates each step with the bass drum. True to the live version, the metallophone intro is without bass (because Umberto could not play both at the same time). The whole martial song structure is laid out twice instrumentally, and only the second time, the bass enters while the guitar does some treble figures. Giovanni starts singing the refrain, first hesitantly and then more securely in the third progression. Then the song enters a slowed down free-form punctuated by the bass drum before Giovanni shouts 'only a therapy' thirty-four times. The record seems to be stuck or defective because the singing doesn't follow the drum kick, which creates a sort of anxious feeling about where this will end. Live, especially in the beginning, Giovanni performed a staged attack on Annarella, dressed as *Italia* in the iconography of Italian unification process; she defended herself and hit back to what looks like a simulated rape. The song then continues as if nothing had happened, and towards the end, Giovanni is able to vocalize in a way that reminds of his childhood as Catholic boarding school choir boy. Curami ends with an 'I', a rare case in Italian but common in Latin, and therefore, the word probably reminded him of Latin church singing.

Lyrically, this is a prime example of Giovanni's fascination with mental health on one hand and with care on a more affective dimension. He sings in fact both 'cure me' as an imperative to healing and 'take care of me', which might even mean 'cuddle me' and that he alternates with minimal variations in word letters (a classic Giovanni's trick) into an institutional 'take me into your care'. As said, Giovanni started the band after five years as caretaker/psychiatric operator in a mental institution, an experience which had left him burned out and in need of some kind of care himself. In Berlin, the band was feeling the harshness of the cold, dark city in the winter, but at the same time, the solidarity and openness of squatters, audiences, and night revellers in squats, discos, and clubs. These were sort of taking care of the band, providing them with food, a warm shelter, and lively dancing audiences.

The lyrics then obscurely refer to 'helms' and 'new weapons' that an unknown enemy might use to strike back. The first free associations this builds in my mind is with a filmic fascination of the band: *Aguirre, the Wrath of God* (1972), whose protagonist Klaus Kinski resembles Giovanni a lot in terms of features. The film is also dominated by a semi-invisible enemy army terrorizing and bringing the Spanish crew in the Amazons to the verge of madness.

'Mi Ami? (Remiscelata)' is a remixed version of the song which appeared on the EP *Ortodossia II* in 1985. It seems to simply have more punch and to be equalized better but no major remixing has been performed. Literature scholar and writer Rossi (2024) refers to the fact that Massimo came up with the incipit inspired by translating wrongly *Blue Erections,* the English title of a film on a poster outside an X-rated cinema in Reggio. By looking at the sad faces of his fellow inhabitants, he imagined that their hard-ons were probably as 'blue', meaning as 'sad', as the ones the film title was referring to.

The drum machine and the guitar open the song with a simple mid-tempo 'doo-wop' (I–vi–IV–V) chord progression in C major, while the bass plays a catchy melody in its higher frets.

Giovanni then starts distantly crooning about a sad erection, indifferent sperms, both modest and molest intercourses and indigest swallowing. This is a song about some kind of love, misplacing the romantic with the erotic, in a clinical 'cold-pop' way, like what DAF were doing in several of their songs, including 'Liebe auf den ersten Blick' ('Love at first sight') and 'Sex unter Wasser' ('Sex underwater'), or Gang of Four with their song 'Damaged Goods'. All these bands were consciously subtracting the singer from any vocally performed involvement, as in a kind of dissociation. Giovanni achieves this by using only the neutral scientific words for sexual acts, ridiculing them with a sometime odd, sometime humorous use of adjectives.

When I asked the music writer and critic Fabio de Luca about 1960s influences on 'Mi Ami', he told me that:

> In general, the return of interest in 1960s songs in the early 1980s came after a season of very sharp break with that moment in history, coinciding with the politicised 1970s, where the disengaged song was regarded with suspicion if not open disapproval. Recovering 'Saint Tropez twist' or 'Nessuno Mi Può Giudicare'[3] in 1982 was an attempt to reconnect with the last collective 'serene' moment of which one vaguely had memory, almost an evocation of an archetype. Because let us remember that even the 1980s, before becoming the yuppie paradise they would be after 1985, were a season of great uncertainty and therefore fear: with the traditional economy in crisis, with the long tail of terrorism, with the spread of heroin, with the unstable scenarios of the Cold War.... For Ferretti and the others –

---

[3] Hits from the 1960s, sung, respectively, by Peppino di Capri and Caterina Caselli.

> precisely because they were from Emilia – the relationship with *il liscio* had never ceased, it was something in which they were immersed and which belonged to them throughout their childhood and adolescence, it was DNA: so, there was no nostalgia, not even unconscious. In this, perhaps CCCP were the least retro thing that ever came out in Italy.
>
> (De Luca 2024)

De Luca distinguishes CCCP from bands such as Righeira and Gruppo Italiano, who were reconnecting to the 1960s with a nostalgic and revivalist spirit. True that CCCP wanted to go beyond 1960s romantic love, and according to Michele Rossi, they wanted to show how a 'love story is always an enigma, a journey without a destination. And if we do not look for what we love, we only settle for what we find on the road' (Rossi 2024).

Once the song starts accelerating and distortion kicks in, Giovanni's crooning turns into his usual frantic screaming, and the text tells of a different kind of love, a love put under the semiotic lens. Giovanni grabs a copy of Roland Barthes' *Fragments d'un discours amoureux* ('Fragments of a lover's discourse', 1977), a theoretical treaty about love that was widely popular in Italy at the time (Einaudi published it as a paperback in 1977), especially among DAMS students such as himself, and performs a sort of cut-up of sub-chapters and quotes stating that love is a rapture, an ecstasy and 'absolute tranquillity' and repeatedly asking 'do you love me?' in the refrain. As in 'Curami', also 'Mi ami?' ends with an 'I', therefore allowing a religious Latinesque chanting melody.

But this is not all, 'stop talking, come a little closer', the coda of the song, offers a third understanding of love, a kind of awkward and twee kind of love, an invitation to stop overthinking and overtalking and just relax, a farcical situation for every shy nerd overpowered by simplicity. Interestingly, the nature of this love in terms of gender remain obscure, apart from the reference to an erection in the beginning. Despite this song and despite the sometime highly erotic conduct of Annarella and Fatur onstage, CCCP remain a very asexual band, with no hints of rockist sexuality, patriarchal logics, and female objectification. There is some kind of libidinal suppression in the band, that is let free only via the dancers/performers and that is otherwise contained, hidden, and repressed. Giovanni is mostly responsible for this, embodying to this day a religious, ascetic, celibate figure both on- and off-stage. The other musicians also maintained a 'cold-pop' demeanour in clear opposition to Annarella and Fatur.

*'Trafitto'* means 'pierced', 'transfixed'. The song has a plain structure based on an initial acoustic guitar arpeggio, followed by a simple Oi! punk midtempo riff, very close to UK Subs' 'Warhead'. The drums play along programmed like an unassuming drummer would play; it seems to be the most faithful reproduction of Zeo's drumming, including some tom rolls. The song then suddenly gathers momentum by intensifying the drumming and changing riff, while Giovanni accumulates images about a so-called democratic era before returning to the mid-tempo and to a sort of coda. As often with CCCP, the song has an unconventional structure. Bratus (2024) refers to the fact that CCCP worked with progressive intensification (based on accented acceleration and compression of rhythmic values) and syntagmatic repetition and sees this as the stylistic trademark of the band in its early period.

The lyrics stand out because they don't have the typical word games, cutouts, and repetitions of Giovanni's writing nor the irony of Massimo. Giovanni (Ob&k 2015c) said that the lyrics were given to them as a kind of present by a cousin of Massimo after a gig. Umberto states that

> it was a song that came from a riff of mine, very sad, very…
> a love story gone wrong, etcetera, etcetera. We mixed it with
> this text, which was a poem by Massimo's famous cousin, the
> one who had introduced us to each other.
>
> (Negri 2023b)

'Trafitto' is an impressionistic take on the 1980s; it gathers images of a collective defeat, where the lyrical 'I' remembers about well-rounded and reasonable speeches and where we are still siding with revolt, despite the fact that this democratic era seems to lead elsewhere. There is also a desire for closeness, for a person that would be a pillow in a kind of longing that is, however, seen as fragile.

Lasting a little more than a minute, 'Valium Tavor Serenase' might be CCCP's manifesto, at least of their early years. It was already performed by MitropaNK and might be one of the first songs that Giovanni and Massimo worked on. The song hits with one single repeated power chord and Giovanni's frantic phrasing, over and over again as in a hardcore intro, until opening up to a simple UK punk riff, modifying it into an ascending furious one, stopping to make space to a deconstructed version of liscio's most celebrated song 'Romagna Mia', reprising the punk riff and closing before the listener has had time to realize what had just happened. The drum machine also reproduces quite faithfully Zeo's drumming style.

But first things first: Valium, Tavor, and Serenase are three brand labels for Diazepam, an anxiolytic; Lorazepam, a medication for anxiety; and Haloperidol, an antipsychotic.

According to Fatur (2023), Giovanni in his time as a psychiatric operator had the task of administering these medicines to patients. The song is therefore on one hand a snapshot on Giovanni's professional every day and the one of his patients, and on the other, a programmatic take on mixing punk with Emilian melodic music. The lyrics tell of the medicines' effects and then address or, better, attack a plural 'you' with existential questions and with antithetical alternatives, trying to justify and make sense on one hand the use (or abuse?) of medicines and, on the other, of subcultural practices, like having green hair.

'Romagna Mia' is one of the most well-known songs of liscio. Secondo Casadei composed and recorded it in 1954 as a homage to his land ('Romagna Mia', n.d.). Since then, it has grown in popularity all around Italy and features in the repertoire of several music ensembles, often requested in liscio dance floors. Giovanni sings a part of the lyrics but, then with a simple but effective detournement, changes 'Romagna' to 'Emilia'. As we noted in the first chapter, Emilia-Romagna is a hyphenated region in Italy, with a strong inner rivalry.

Moreover, at least in my own brief experience as social operator and special education teacher in nursing homes and schools, liscio represent a kind of soundtrack to social work. Simple melodic music on the radio is something that both operators and patients can cope with, in similar ways as in supermarkets, public festivals, and other places. In relation to liscio's German counterpart, *Schlager*, Mendívil (2016, 102) affirms that 'German schlager artists construct a particular German community by singing about emotions that are considered to be familiar, affirmative and crucial to a positive life. Central to these emotions are love, friendship and the love of Heimat'. These are the same features that make liscio such a significant medication to cope with mental distress because it provides a useful calming effect by providing an obvious, familiar, and optimistic image to long for. Funnily enough Giovanni sings the verse of the song about longing for a *casolare*, another way to refer to a farmhouse, such as the one he was inhabiting in Fellegara and that provided CCCP's rehearsal space and creative headquarters.

Closing side A of the LP is 'Morire' ('Dying'), CCCP's first attempt in making their way sonically towards the Far East. A highly effected acoustic guitar plays a Japanese-music influenced melody, trying to imitate a shamisen, over a simple harmonic structure provided by a bass arpeggio. Massimo provides one of his best guitar performances ever, and despite the possible accusation of orientalism, there is an undeniable respectful atmosphere arising from the song. Giovanni's voice, initially filtered through the studio reverb plate that creates distance, tells of an epochal defeat and of an existential paradox: Dying is unbearable for those who cannot really live. Once the distorted guitar kicks in, the lyrics homage two writers by naming them: the Russian poet Vladimir Mayakovsky and the Japanese author Yukio Mishima. Both born on the eve of the 1920s but ideologically opposite artists committed suicide. Both were also significant presences on the bookshelves of any respectable provincial intellectual, conveying an ideal of desperate but heroic existence as tormented poet. The song has probably the longest intro without drums. However, once the bass designs an angular and intricated riff, the drum machine appears with a frantic *motorik*, and the guitar starts drawing distorted free forms and the usual grattugiare, while Giovanni handles down to posterity some of his most iconic words: '*produci consuma crepa*' (produce, consume, die). Today, these words cover walls all over Italy and were recently seen on a banner in an automobile industry workers' strike, as in a picture featured on *Newsweek* ('Tens of Thousands of Italian Autoworkers Join First Strike in 20 Years – Newsweek', n.d.). However, this simple triparted bland life under capitalism is also compared to a life outside of it, be it the one of a drug-addicted person looking for a shot or the one of a punk working on his hairdo and studs, ending either way in death. The sentence about cutting your hair and dying of boredom is close to a similar verse, in German, on Fehlfarben's 'Gottseidank Nicht in England' (*Monarchie und Alltag*, 1980). CCCP and Massimo, in particular, liked Fehlfarben and often covered 'Militürk' from the same album (Bottin 2024), but this might simply be a kind of casual attuning in subcultural narration more than a homage or a rip off. The song ends with a female voice, probably Annarella, punctuating the word *crepa* accompanied by a slowing down snare drum.

## *Side B*

'Noia' (Boredom) is a kind of soft landing into the B side of the album. Boredom is at the heart of the modern art experience (Haladyn 2015). About popular music, geographer Anderson (2021, 200) notes how:

> (b)oredom was regularly invoked in UK punk as part of a critique of the monotony and vapidity of Fordism and working-class life, or rather the empty time of a life divided into stable work and compensatory leisure at the cusp of the neoliberal counterrevolution.

Punk feared boredom as embedded in normality and opposed it with a frenzy, amphetamine-fuelled stimulation, with do-it-yourself industriousness, and with loud and uncompromising noise. CCCP seemed not to buy this; their boredom is existential and it is something that Giovanni associate with normality and mortality. CCCP indulge in boredom, use it as a creative strategy to dig into existence as a whole, and this puts them in overt contradiction with the punk ethos.

The drum machine plays a simple pattern rhythm, while the bass plays a descending line, reminiscent of the goth music of the time, and the guitar let out feedback. All is engulfed by reverb, the same kind that was applied on Giovanni's voice on 'Morire'.

About halfway though the song, once the reverb is lifted and the song kicks in, Giovanni sings *noia*, the title, with an elaborated chant, clearly inspired by Catholic sacred music he was performing in the nun-run boarding school he attended as a child and that left an immense influence on his singing but also world-view. 'Noia', is stretched in a similar way as 'amen' in a Catholic mass, the formula used at the end of prayers.

Slowly, the arrangement detracts elements, and the bass simply punctuates the chords, giving space to the chaos in the back; the guitar continues to work with free-form, and for the second time in the album, we can hear female voices (Silvia and Annarella) screaming in the back, together with feedback and something which might be a saxophone. Giovanni repeats the first verse, and the song ends with his voice, alone, chanting again the elaborated refrain consisting only of the word *noia*.

There is basically no pause in between, and we immediately hear Massimo playing an irresistible simple drone-like riff of one note with octave (very close to Adam and the Ants's 'Xerox') on top of a drum machine with the simple motorik beat accelerating and stabilizing once the bass kicks in to define the three-chord harmony. This is 'Io sto bene' (I feel fine) CCCP's poppiest number that can fill a dance floor in seconds.

The variations in the song are minimal, the bass in the refrain climbs up the neck to the highest notes, the guitar lets out some static noises and some glam-like riffs, but for the most part, this is just a groovy endless ostinato allowing Giovanni to be lyrically as inventive as usual.

A full song about how someone is doing seems to be a very Italian thing. Giovanni addresses this in sociological terms; he refers to everyday routines to their being about quality or being simply a formality, that is, a convention. The climax of the song sees him delivering another (after the one found in 'Morire') iconic verse, nowadays part of Italian folk culture: 'I don't study, I don't work I don't watch TV I don't go to the cinema I don't do sport', words which could be lifted from some questionnaire or census in their essentialism. Sociologist Romania sees this sentence as 'a form of resistance to anomie, flaunting an attitude of voluntary non-participation that today would be defined as NEET (not in education, employment or training) or *hikkikomori*' (Romania 2016, 77). It also again seems to address some kind of boredom, again presented in existential terms. CCCP distance themselves from British and American punk by denying the possibility of 'getting kicks' out of something and diving into a kind if individualist boredom dominated by nothingness.

The song has a fantastic coda, with the guitar finally playing anthemically the three power chords in a kind of Steve Jones or Pete Townshend way, while Annarella and Silvia punctuate the 'I feel fine, I feel bad' in child-like and hypnotic manner.

At this point, no one would have expected a tango, but 'Allarme' (alarm) starts with a bass line accented by the snare drum and leading us back to an Emilian *balera* (dance hall or pavilion), and on top of this, a melodica draws sinister melodic lines trying to imitate what an accordion in a song by Tienno

Pataccini would do. After 'Valium Tavor Serenase', that had a waltz insert, we are back in liscio's territory, in Emilian's own folk music. However, this time, the mood is much darker. The melodica is sometime out of tune, and the bass is martial and staccato, and in the distance, Giovanni recites images of paralysis, partiality, and agitation, where something is reaching a tipping point and seems in the end to collapse or quickly escalate. Once the bass provides a key change, the riff mutates into something even darker, another The Cure/Bauhaus-inspired descending riff effected with some filter and a weird distortion. Back to the tango part, the haunting melodica is layered with found noises and reverbs while the new-wave part returns increasingly noisy and distorted. Giovanni recites again a tense monologue inviting a possible enemy or execution squad to aim for the heart. The new-wave part intensifies with panned noise effects as Giovanni sings *solo tu* (only you or you alone) over and over again.

*Affinità e Divergenze* ends with 'Emilia Paranoica' (paranoid Emilia), here in a *remiscelata* ('remixed') version of the one that appeared on the *Compagni, cittadini, fratelli, partigiani* EP in 1985. The song is a dirge reaching nearly eight minutes in length and belongs to a corpus of songs, representing a sort of 'alternative canon' within punk and post-punk. These genres are in fact dominated by immediacy and briefness, with songs rarely passing three minutes, in defiance of progressive rock music. However, tracks such as Patti Smith Group's 'Land: Horses / Land of a Thousand Dances / La Mer(de)', Bauhaus's 'Bela Lugosi's Dead', Television's 'Marquee Moon', P.I.L.'s 'Theme', Siouxsie and the Banshees's 'Lord's Prayer', The Cure's 'One Hundred Years', and Die Krupps's 'Stahlwerksynfonie', among others, defy this understanding, stretching above seven to eight minutes. Just like these songs, 'Emilia Paranoica' represents the need to work creatively beyond the youthful idea of speed and to affirm and territorialize sound as a more meditative and possibly ecstatic presence.

Giovanni writes about the origin of the song lyrics, as beginning from a 'hammering rhythm in the head and two obsessive words: Emilia paranoica. Nothing else' (Contiero 2015, 13). Back from a car trip to Morocco at night, he is obsessing over writing and only walking up to the second floor of the Fellegara house; he is surprised by the moonlight, and some words start forming in his head as he gets ready for another sleepless night, 'waiting to collapse at dawn' (Contiero 2015, 21). Musically, Massimo and Giovanni were looking for the sound of a steam engine (Campo, Ferretti, & Zamboni 2005, 25); once, they found that a stolen guitar and amp appeared out of the blue in their rehearsal space, and Massimo started strumming a E major chord.

But let's get back to the 'hammering rhythm'; it is close to the one in 'Noia' but differently accented, reminding me of Laurie Anderson's 'Born Never Asked'. The drum machine drives through the song as an ostinato motorik that allows the rest to move and cluster freely, following Giovanni's insomniac lyrics, with only an abrupt acceleration mid-song. In a 1983 interview with DJ Tacco from local Radio Antenna 1, resurfaced on Mixcloud (Tacchini 1983), Giovanni tells how paranoid Emilia is about being in a certain state of mind which is difficult to define but easy to experience; it is about being unsatisfied even if living in a well-administered, civilized, tolerant place.

The song is a kind of post-punk and provincial 'Autobahn', a psycho-geographic journey through Emilia and its paranoia. The lyrics are among Giovanni's most accomplished; a cut-up of existential *ennui*, nightly visions of sleep and restlessness, references to Lebanon's tragic past and present, sadly matching today's situation, and to *Ma l'amor mio non muore* ('But my love doesn't die'), a 1913 silent movie. Carlo Chiapparini recites the opening words, about a 'bitterer cold and dry and tense chords signal your entry in my memory', which are played backwards in the LP version. This enigmatic sentence might refer to the meeting of Giovanni and Massimo in a Berlin club, where, as stated in Chapter 1, coldness was a kind of aesthetic and affective trope or, on a more general level, wants to introduce that atmosphere. Annarella and Silvia scream the title several times, enhancing the same atmosphere, and somehow assigning a gendered dimension to Emilia, which can in fact also be a name for a person.

Moreover, blurred snapshots of subcultural nightlife between intoxication and some kind of club hopping appear. Medicines such as Rohypnol, a benzodiazepine, and Plegine, a kind of amphetamine abused especially in the early 1980s, are mentioned, while *77* was the nickname of a young punk from Sassuolo who briefly played guitar in a local band called Upside. The Tuwat squat and a new ARCI club are also in the song. Giovanni is somehow reporting some inside jokes of the Emilian punk scene. Music works as a kind of live scoring to the lyrics; once Plegine is mentioned there is an abrupt acceleration, as if its euphoric and energizing effects would kick in and lead into a slightly dissociative reflection on oneself and then on a restless moving among Emilian provincial towns, Reggio, Parma, Modena, ending up in the already mentioned Tuwat in Carpi.

Absent in the remiscelata LP version is the sardonic long laugh that Silvia performed. Ignazio Orlando heavily remixed the song, adding delay to the drums and to the bass, as to make the simple structure of the tracks more articulated and percussive, close to industrial. The guitar plays a simple but effective riff panned in stereo, sometimes overlaid by an incisive melody or by free-forms, while the bass draws repetitive rhythmic lines, which are verging on what will be called a decade later, nu-metal, and sometimes abandoning them to perform elegant melodic lines in dialogue with the voice.

The word *paranoica*, declined in multiple ways, takes over the song to its false end and then in the final reprise. The album ends with Giovanni forcefully screaming at the top of his lungs *pa-ra-noi-ca* several times and Umberto's faded-out laugh, who was with him in the singing booth in the studio.

# 3 *Emila Paranoica*: Imaginary and Affective Territorialization from an Italian Province

*Affinità e Divergenze* is all but a punk album. It is a complex and explosive artefact, revealing an original understanding of the role of music and cultural work in society. CCCP were shaking up and destabilizing consolidated ideas about what can be sung about, in which language and where, and which cultural influences are 'natural' and which are not. The record performs an imaginary and affective territorialization by redefining spatial borders, centres and peripheries and areas of cultural and political influence.

## Space and *Terroir*

Interviews with Giovanni and Massimo across the years (De Falchi 2023) show their continuous engaging with the complexity of the world, sometimes entering ambiguous ideological grey zones but mostly revealing an intense fascination with territories and with cultural, social, and economic processes attached to them. On one hand, this fascination is always somehow imaginary as if they and the rest of the band would project their own desires into the less known. However, this also takes an affective dimension in turning places into some kind of *Heimat* and creating a lasting emotional bond, be it based on ideological affinity, paranoia, or both.

Geographer Doreen Massey (2005) conceptualized space not as an empty and static container but as something alive, connected to the presence of others, and encompassing scales from the intimate to the global. Space is both social and relational; it contains myriad stories intersecting with each other; and, it is never finished and is always shifting and changing. However, power always determines how social negotiations work in space, making it intrinsically political. According to Massey, thinking about space in these terms, as inherently dynamic, social, and political, has the ability to foster an ethos of engagement with the world and to challenge grand and linear narratives of historical development, therefore revealing alternative and heterogeneous meanings attached to it.

One way to investigate the 'heterogeneous paths' described by Massey is to introduce the notion of territory and territorialization. A territory can be understood as a dynamic and socially accepted configuration of space, which works simultaneously at the material and imaginative levels. These two dimensions – the material reality and the social narratives – both contribute to its meaning, while also reflecting different regimes of knowledge (Teil 2011). To overcome these static duality, the concept of territorialization is useful. This refers to the continuous process of creating and preserving a territory, establishing boundaries, structure, and meaning within ever-changing space. This process often involves the provision of strong cultural and even 'magical' imagined elements, as exemplified by the concept of *terroir*. Terroir represents both a material and complex interaction of soils, microclimate, grapes, and human senses and work, as well as a social construct based on narratives about these material elements. The word is also increasingly used outside the narrow borders of wine production to express complex dynamics surrounding locality (Demossier 2016).

Many of the creative strategies employed by CCCP echo these understandings of space in its heterogeneous and political dimensions and of territorialization as the attempt to colonize and impose meaning on it. Emerging from a provincial context, the band engages with grand narratives concerning Europe, rock music, punk and subcultures, and world powers. They approach these narratives in spatial terms, recognizing their artificial and power-dependent origins. The band destabilizes established territories by building an alternative socio-spatial, musical, and cultural space, where distances and differences are sometimes obnoxiously reduced and moulded into their own grand narrative. However, this massive emotional engagement with space occurs through minimal and very precarious means, thereby subverting consolidated understandings of power and hegemony. Moreover, these spaces become the terroir, defining CCCP's work and providing them with a unique aura in the Italian musical scene.

I will look at a few of these narratives of terroir and the way they are played out in *Affinità e Divergenze*, starting from the most obvious: the province.

## CCCP and the *Provincia*

The only real terroir of *Affinità e Divergenze* is the smelly manured land surrounding the farmhouse in Fellegara. This is where the band and its world-views came to be, this is where they rehearsed, and this is where they perfected their sound and unusual song structure. This is also where Giovanni read compulsively, stared at maps, and penned most of his lyrics. This is also a kind of place that any Italian would understand as *provinciale*.

The idea of the *provincia* in Italian has an administrative and a cultural connotation. Administratively, Italy is divided secularly into regions, provinces, and municipalities. However, provincia has also a more subtle connotation, implying a marginal, subaltern positioning in relation to bigger urban centres. The province is at the same time a quiet and authentic place, with specific traditions related especially to food and language, but at the same time, implying backwardness, immobility, and boredom.

There is a corpus of films and novels describing the limits of the province and the lure that big urban centres have, especially on young people, such as Luciano Bianciardi's novels *Il Lavoro Culturale* (1957) and *La Vita Agra* (1962), available in English as *It's a Hard Life*. The difference between city and province spatializes a temporal divide between outward modernity and inward conservatism. The province is therefore always understood as arriving late not only to huge societal transformations but also in relation to trends, which quickly spread in urban centres.

However, in the 1980s, according to musicologist Jacopo Tomatis (2021), the new Italian rock music settles in the provinces, materially, thanks to fanzines and small independent labels but also from the point of view of the imaginary. Among the first examples is Pordenone where the Great Complotto gathered local punk bands into a vital and creative scene. Tomatis, however, considers the case of Vasco Rossi as most significant, who to today is probably the biggest Italian rock star. Vasco quickly became the embodiment of provincial ennui, that he thematizes as a collective us against the world, with 'us' made up of marginal losers.

CCCP are also proudly provincial as already seen in Chapter 1, and as Tomatis says, 'non-accidentally Emilian', just like Vasco. Tracing a line from Vasco to Giovanni seems nearly blasphemous because the first is the king of mainstream rock and the second the most improbable rock star of the country. However, in both cases, we find the use of the same terroir, which becomes the green screen for the projection of very different spatial and cultural imaginaries, references, and desires; this is performed statically in the case of Vasco and dynamically in the case of CCCP.

Provincia exists in its indeterminacy; it is a kind of spatial ethos (Krims 2007), a way to talk about and make sense of the marginal and the non-urban in the Italian context, where diverse marginal spaces of various entity and sometime contrasting imaginaries can coexist without mutually excluding each other. Provincials are Alpine valleys, the Sicilian hinterland, Emilian towns and Milan's metropolitan conurbation; it all depends on where from you are looking at them and what you project on them.

This external and power-related labelling of what province is and what it is not is somehow also liberating. In its indeterminacy, the province allows for experimentations and creative elain, which cities either suffocate through conformity or deliberately exploit. CCCP members have always been proudly provincial, even in their very expected detournement, where Reggio becomes supposedly the centre of the world. Helena Velena describes them to me as *provincialotti*, simple provincial guys, but still in the lineage of local Communist partisans and, therefore, somehow true to their values and world-views (Velena 2024).

The logic behind CCCP's imaginary and affective territorialization is always a provincial logic, developing a particular kind of nostalgia (that I here refer to as *Ostalgie*), which shapes their musical production and the stories they attach to it. It is this marginal condition that allows them not to take for granted their own terroir but to reimagine it and reterritorialize it into a plural and complex cultural and geographical crucible, very much based on somewhere else they long for. This operation is of course a construct, therefore able to be read, interpreted, and understood but also instrumentalized in, once again, diverse and contrasting ways.

In the next sections, I will try to make sense of this theoretical understanding by referring to the way CCCP adopt and adapt Ostalgie, how they operate with maximalism, and how their work can be understood under the framework of the off-modern.

## *Ostalgie*

The entrance to the *Felicitazioni!* exhibition in Reggio Emilia left me puzzled: a *Trabant* car surrounded by *cheval de frise*, a pole with megaphones and a small portion of the Berlin Wall, occupied the middle of first cloister of the exhibition space, while national flags from Eastern Bloc republics hung from the porches' ceilings. What kind of atmosphere were they trying to convey here? Portions of the Berlin wall ended up anywhere from a Las Vegas bathroom to a concrete factory in Veneto, while *Trabis* (as they were familiarly known) have been turned into toy souvenirs or can be driven around Berlin in urban safaris. Next to me, fans of the band rejoiced and took pictures.

It therefore didn't come as a surprise that CCCP performed three sold-out shows (24, 25, and 26 February 2024) in Astra Kulturhaus in Berlin under the high-in-consonants title CCCP IN DDDR. After the already-mentioned exhibition and grand gala in Reggio Emilia (see Introduction), this was the third instance of their reformation. The added D in DDR meant 'dissolved', as explained in the poster.

About 4500 people over three nights, mostly travelling from all over Italy, flocked to the R.A.W. Gelände, an industrial location, surrounded by railway tracks in the former East Berlin district of Friedrichshain, some of them safe in the belief that the band belonged there and that that was their territory, even their terroir. As seen in Chapter 1, CCCP built much of their image and reputation on the connection to Berlin, where Giovanni and Massimo met, where they played their first well-received gigs, and where they experienced punk and NDW bands making new and cold music in German. However, all this was happening in West Berlin, while their visits to the Eastern side of the city were limited to one-day tourist visas and little interaction with the locals. Punk was highly repressed, controlled, and monitored in the GDR, sometimes with band members and hangers-on serving prison sentences (Mohr 2018).

The band had indeed played in the Eastern Bloc, in Moscow and Saint Petersburg (at the time, Leningrad) in 1989, as part of a delegation of Italian bands, after a few Russian bands had played in a music festival in Melpignano (D'Alife and Mariani 2023), but that remained mostly limited to a kind of official cultural exchange imbued in soft diplomacy and came right at the end of CCCP's (to be understood both as the band and the Soviet Union) experience.

A real interaction with the Eastern Bloc is therefore minimal, although CCCP from their name to their martial appearance in uniforms on-stage, from their pro-Soviet declarations in interviews to their narrated world-view, felt absolutely part of that territory. Explaining this by simply referring to post-modern irony is not enough. In my view, CCCP in *Affinità e Divergenze* performed all of this as Ostalgie.

Ostalgie is a combination of *Ost*, German for East and *Nostalgie*, nostalgia, apparently invented by Uwe Steimle, a cabaret actor from Dresden. Since the early 1990s a variety of cultural phenomena, artefacts and practices, and commercial endeavours have been labelled with this term, ranging from films, such as *Good Bye Lenin!* (Wolfgang Becker, 2003) to retro parties, from beer labels to T-shirts reproducing or getting inspiration from symbols and brands of GDR's origin. Other terms have surfaced in relation to a wider post-Soviet nostalgia (Kalinina 2014), and localized for instance with Yugo-Nostalgia (Volčič 2007) in the ex-Yugoslavia and with PRL nostalgia (Golinowska 2016) in Poland.

Nonetheless, I prefer to use Ostalgie, in German, and in its wider reference to a general 'East', which might be used in scalar ways from *East* Berlin to the whole *Eastern* Bloc. Moreover, Soviet nostalgia has lately acquired a more sinister meaning because of the current aggressive Russian foreign policy.

Social scientist and journalist Thomas Ahbe writes that

> *Ostalgie* handles in an amateurish way the average East German perspective on an important rupture in experience: the peaceful revolution and the introduction of West German conditions in East Germany. *Ostalgie* is not a depiction of history, it does not have missionary zeal, and it does not oblige anyone to be informed, educated, convinced or

edified. *Ostalgie* is instead self-centred, it is self-assurance and self-therapy. *Ostalgie* is a matter of amateurs. As this is a lay discourse, it is also imprecise, indirect, contradictory, ironic and unserious.

(Ahbe 2005, 44)

Ahbe therefore sees it as generated by East Germans within a specific period; however, he also traces some aspects of it which are useful to my analysis. In the already-mentioned recording of the live in UFA-Fabrik 1985 in West Berlin (Le Dinamiche 2023), during 'Live in Pankow', Annarella gets on stage in what looks like a sombre dark blue 1950s lady's suit complete with hat, lifts her left fist, and starts waving a flag of the GDR, while Giovanni sings about East European capitals and finding shelter under the Warsaw Pact. He is himself dressed as a *VoPo*. I argue here that what CCCP were doing there was performing Ostalgie. First because they are thematizing the East as in Eastern Bloc and doing it in the West. Paradoxically, their show would have been unacceptable a few kilometres east from the UFA-Fabrik, behind the Wall, in 1985. Moreover, they perform it with a kind of nostalgic elain. Annarella is dressed in a conservative, nearly Weimar republic style; her look is stern; and she waves the flag in a composed way, transmitting a sense of pathos and authority. This is the same kind of feel that we get from the cover of *Affinità e Divergenze*, from the band's logo, from their fascination for army boots and caps, and from some of the lyrics of 'CCCP' where Giovanni lists East European official newspapers. This is an Ostalgie that is, however, different than Ahbe's post-1989 definition, canonised by popular culture, and is somehow more faithful to its name. Nostalgia is in fact born as a spatial condition not a temporal one, and it should least be understood as framed by a particular spatial-temporal atmosphere, where longing is pervasive and distance seems immensurable.

Moreover, as ethnographer Dominic Boyer suggests:

> Ostalgie is not what it seems to be – it is a symptom less of East German nostalgia than of West German utopia. I mean utopia in the sense that it is a naturalizing fantasy that creates an *irrealis* space, literally a 'no-place', in which East Germans' neurotic entanglement with authoritarian pastness allows those Germans gendered western to claim a future free from the burden of history.
>
> (Boyer 2006, 363)

If we open this up, we can see how *Affinità e Divergenze* and CCCP as a project are in fact exactly working on an imagined and imaginary attempt at territorializing a space they cannot access directly through sounds and images which are condemned to a nostalgic elain. The reason for doing this can be understood as twofold. First, it lies in the post-1977 condition of being transfixed by the future and by 1980s consumerism (as in 'CCCP' and 'Trafitto') and dealing with the end of utopian and ideological thinking. Second, CCCP are longing for a place, where life is not only mere producing, consuming, and dying ('Morire') and where they can be taken care of ('Curami') and loved ('Mi Ami?').

# A Big Map of the USSR: Maximalism Versus Minimalism

According to Massimo's recollection (Campo, Ferretti, & Zamboni 2005, 37), Giovanni had a gigantic map of Asia hanging on the wall in Fellegara. This is also visible in a picture (Contiero 2015, 68).

Imagining the band 'eyeballing' such a map might provide some context to what CCCP were thinking: Asia is covered in its entirety by Soviet, Mongolian, and Chinese territories, with Europe representing a tiny peninsula. Giovanni was probably intrigued by the spaces exhibited in the map, rich in cultural diversity but, at the same time, ruled by common political faith in socialism. He saw that gigantic portion of the Earth reaching west towards Reggio Emilia and towards Fellegara where the map was hanging. Totalitarianism mesmerized him. As already noted, interviews with him are rich in references to Islam, the Austro-Hungarian Empire, the Soviet Union, Mongolian Empire, and China (De Falchi 2023). These are the territories that matter to CCCP, first and foremost as spatial and second as cultural entities. Spatially, they are huge and size matters to CCCP. The red banner they were taking around in the beginning of their career, the one with a light tower and CCCP written under it, was enormous and sometimes the trio of black-clad 'students' with interesting haircuts looked inadequate in front of it (see Figure 1.2). It was only by adding performers to the live show that their maximalist plan started to take form.

Second, the band is mesmerized by the cultural variety of the aforementioned totalitarian empires that they explored both as listeners and as performers. CCCP take influences from Japanese, Islamic, Korean, and Lebanese music very seriously; they overcome a simple accusation of orientalism by embracing cultures in their ideological dimension and by investing intellectual capital in them.

This kind of operation is not always successful and devoid of colonial simplifications. For instance, in 1985 they participate to a national television show called *Obladì Obladà* directed by Serena Dandini. Their video contribution, directed by Renato De Maria, is mostly filmed in Tuwat in Carpi and in its surroundings, and the band attempts at playing all their cards at once. It includes a scene with Annarella, Silvia, and a third person covered in Niqāb and screaming from a balcony, next to someone in a border guard uniform, and another scene where Silvia is performing martial art moves and Annarella showcases Maoist fashion behind the band performing 'Morire' in Soviet uniforms. One way to make sense of this complexity is to refer to CCCP's aesthetics as maximalist. Maximalism has been used both as a political and an art-related concept, with very different connotations. According to political thinker Antonio Gramsci (1925), it refers to a fatalist 'all or nothing' stance within the Communist party, which sees the Marxian victory of the proletariat as a certain and absolute end result, therefore relativizing any possible small and partial progress towards it. Comparative literature scholar Stefano Ercolino defines maximalism in literature as characterized by 'length, encyclopaedic mode, dissonant chorality, diegetic exuberance, completeness, narratorial omniscience, paranoid imagination, inter-semiocity, ethical commitment, and hybrid realism' (Ercolino 2012, 242) and refers in particular to the work of authors such as Thomas Pynchon, David Foster Wallace, and Zadie Smith.

As said, size, in terms of political expectations and of literary production, matters. CCCP in *Affinità e Divergenze* declare themselves as Togliatti's children, and they fantasize about vast territories and adopt and adapt stylistic genre conventions from a variety of music from all over the world. All this fits into a maximalist definition. Of the features selected by Ercolino, length, dissonant chorality, and paranoid imagination fits at best the lyrics and sound that CCCP produced in the LP. However, the way they are trying to achieve this is through technical means that are minimal.

Paradoxically, CCCP's ability to build a maximalist landscape of Italian origin is based on a minimalist, amateurish approach, and, therefore, able to inspire more musical action born under the same circumstances. CCCP were able to overcome punk populism that was identifying a single enemy, building a one-sided opposition, and reproducing simple musical tropes of Anglo-American origin. CCCP were pointing at the complexity of reality and the diversity of forces that were shaping the present and the future more than simple juxtaposing an 'empire of evil' versus us. However, they were doing it with simple, sometimes primitive means involving drum machines, entry-level Japanese guitars, and old used clothes.

## CCCP and the Off-Modern

There is a last significant point which becomes evident when listening to *Affinità e Divergenze*. The band was building a sonic resistance to globalization by relying on modernity, as a trans-European experience. The band refused to use English and even the word *remixed* is Italianized into *remiscelata*. The practice of Italianizing commonly used foreign words was last used during the Fascist dictatorship and surely the band is aware of this. However, they frame it as anti-imperialistic stance and as inspired by the bands they witnessed in Berlin using exclusively German in interviews and in materials attached to records.

The drift between CCCP and the other Italian punk bands (Tosoni and Zuccalà 2020) is built mostly on the former's awareness of the existential tensions of the modern world. CCCP deny Anglo-American influences in their music by referring to Europe as a modern cultural project which was ideologically divided but still alive. Looking at the East in its various geopolitical manifestations is used rhetorically as an antidote to cultural imperialism, which was imposing an ideological consumeristic view on reality thanks to TV shows, commercials, popular culture, and in the postmodern 'art world'.

Academic Frederic Jameson (1991) saw postmodernism as a cultural phenomenon reflecting the logic of late capitalism in aesthetic and economic terms. A lack of depth and linear grand narratives and a tendency towards pastiche of past styles dominate postmodern style in visual arts, literature, and architecture. Moreover, commodification takes over the production of art, which is eventually financialized and devoid of any transformative connotation.

CCCP and Giovanni in particular like to talk about playing 'musica moderna' (Gasparini 1989), and modernity seems to be a wider preoccupation in Giovanni's thoughts. Modernity killed the long Middle Age he still experienced as a child (Maccioni 2013) but also provided the means to enter into a dialogue with the twentieth century in all its dramatic unfolding. CCCP are committed to defend modernity as a project from postmodern logics, affirming authenticity and maintaining art as a safe space for the elaboration of individual and collective trauma.

They also identify the mainstream cultural industry, in Adornoian terms, as the place they aspire to be. Their signing for Virgin Records after the release of *Affinità e Divergenze* should be seen as more proof of their attachment to modernity, not only as an aesthetic project but also as a structure of work.

Punk eroded the border between spectator and performer by giving the illusion that anyone can perform and opening the stage to invasions, sing-alongs, and pogoing (Hebdige 2012). CCCP strictly separated the stage as space for performance from the audience by pulling barbed wire, sometimes metaphorically (Campo, Ferretti, & Zamboni 2005, 49), sometimes for real, on stage. However, their take on modernity cannot be fully understood in terms of faithfulness to a line or absolutism; they recognize that the line can also not be there for real (as they sing in 'CCCP'), and they are aware of the potentials embedded in going off the beaten track.

This is the reason why the off-modern (Boym 2017) might be the most suitable label to make sense of CCCP. While reading this late essay, published after the author's passing, I could not stop thinking about *Affinità e Divergenze*. According to Boym, the off-modern represents a 'detour in to the unexplored potentials of the modern project' (Boym 2017, 3), a 'lateral move' (p. 4) based on 'disorientations', which reveal 'missed opportunities and roads not taken' (p. 5). This concept does not engage with the modern/postmodern duality and moves to the side in search for alternative modernities, eccentric geographies, and human error.

The affective and imaginary territorialization towards the East, the band's lack of ironic distancing but stern human engagement with cultures, which exist beyond the West, and their attention towards avant-gardes of the whole twentieth century means that CCCP were able to foresee that soon punk's no future would become capitalist realism (Fisher 2022), that is, the inability to imagine anything outside and beyond capitalism.

*Affinità e Divergenze* works as a catalogue of alternative modern ways to read reality; it shows that naked sweaty bodies can live with drum machines, liscio with gothic rock and metallophones with distorted guitars; that bass can play melodies and lyrics can be as profound chanted as shouted. It accounts of vast territories, where Emilia is not a province but a whole world and where a band can answer a banal question such as 'Where do you want to get to?' with a sardonic 'To China, through Siberia' (Tondelli 2024, 67).

# Conclusions
Post-Punk and Trans-European Cultural Sensibilities

I wrote this book with someone who cannot understand the lyrics of *Affinità e Divergenze* in mind, just like when I was a young teenager and first heard my favourite British bands. I spent my youth mostly unbothered by understanding lyrics. Lyrics were for me only viable in the music context; they were part of the sound of a band and what made them interesting to me was the singer's 'grain of the voice', the melodies and the general sound, the noisier the better. I discovered new music mostly like this, trusting the way a band sounded or the way they looked in pictures in music magazines. Lyrics were always somehow secondary, apart from the occasional refrain or sentence which stood out; sometimes lyrics were also plain disappointing once I was able to read them.

As established here, CCCP are very much part of the post-punk world (Reynolds 2006). They have a drum machine which is sometimes realistically impersonating a drummer and sometimes is maxed out to its most machine-like expression; they have bass lines, which range from the angular to the melodic; punky guitar parts that can suddenly become free-form abstract noise; and then the voice, torn between shouting and chanting, but always present, always above the rest, even when filtered out and murmuring. Moreover, they are a band which can actually make people dance, as they themselves aspired to.

There is a scene in episode four of Luca Guadagnino's HBO and Sky Atlantic miniseries *We Are Who We Are* (2020), where, surprisingly to all Italian viewers, 'Emilia Paranoica' plays in a wild house party. The series is set in 2016 in a U.S. military base in Chioggia, Italy, and follows the life of American expat teenagers and young military recruits. While CCCP's song is playing, these youngsters, partly undressed because of a swimming pool dive, are dancing, drinking, taking drugs, and heavily flirting. The percussive dimension of the song leads the bacchanal, the main protagonist banging furiously on the walls while the song accelerates, fairly like what Fatur and Annarella were doing onstage. In the live compilation, *CCCP – Fedeli Alla Linea – Live In Punkow* 1996, Giovanni introduces 'Io Sto Bene' by saying 'we really like messing with your heads, but we would rather make you dance'. This is what Guadagnino's teenagers are doing; they are dancing and in doing so they are also performing a lot of what 'Emilia Paranoica' is about. This happens as a pure response to music, not based on only lyrics. They cannot understand the lyrics, but they can get what the song is about. I think that this affective dimension makes *Affinità e Divergenze* a unique album in the Italian context of the 1980s.

As Massimo Volume's singer and poet Emidio Clementi puts it:

> at the time I remember that... we teenagers were firmly convinced that we were living in the wrong place and the big regret was that we weren't born in the United States or in England, where there was more of a connection with rock, where it was a whole other world compared to Italy

and where people were used to hearing distorted guitars. When CCCP came along, however, with that record, which at the time was quite incredible in terms of strength, it put us all a little bit, I wasn't even playing yet, I was playing in an absolutely amateurish way, but it put us in front of a responsibility, the responsibility that we could do the same in Italy, with a different landscape, with a setting that was ours,... clearly Italian, with singing in Italian, and at that point it was no longer a matter of regret that we were born somewhere else. We had to do things because we understood that there was a possibility, that we could be charming in some sexy way, even with what we had with the means we had because then the record wasn't even that you could carry on the idea that 'ah but imagine the fancy studios where they recorded'; they were musicians limited from a technical point of view, the record sounded rough but that became all we wanted to do.

(Clementi 2024)

*Affinità e Divergenze* brought onto the Italian scene a completely new 'post-punk' sensibility. This is first based on experimentalism and a direct ability to work out a variety of musical and cultural influences in a unique way and with care. CCCP are a band which was equally from (West) Berlin as it was from Reggio Emilia, from Fellegara as from Bologna. They were able to project their own provincial identity onto vast unknown areas of the world, territorializing them in affective and imaginary ways. Moreover, they were doing this with sparce means, led only by a strong belief in what they were doing.

This record interplays between maximalism and minimalism; it seems imposing with a fifteen-word title but was recorded in a small cellar. By doing so, it creates huge expectations that it is only partially fulfilling. As journalist and DJ Fabio De Luca writes:

> CCCP were to the Italian eighties what Area were to the 1970s. I only saw them live once, at the *Festa de l'Unità* in Genoa, in September 1986.... I remember the concert as chaotic – of course! – but above all I remember the feeling that none of the various scenes present – the old punks, the goths, the new-wavers, the fashionistas, the *kommunists*, the *Tondelliani*[1] like me – had found, on that stage, what they were looking for. Sending you home laden but dissatisfied, forced to look better within yourself what it was foolish to think you could find there. If that wasn't punk (and DIY) enough....
>
> (De Luca 2024)

Moreover, for many Italian punks, CCCP remained an enigma. Marcello Ganassini, affiliated with Milanese punk at that time, talks nowadays about

> a marked idiosyncrasy between the accidental (and perhaps even somewhat ornamental) absolutism of the Reggiani and the Milanese conjugation of the punk movement. Ferretti's mystical-political deviations, three decades later, are a sort of posthumous seal to two *Weltanschauungen* that could not be together even under torture.
>
> (Ganassini 2024)

CCCP's post-punk sensibility can also reflect in this kind of disappointment and open contrast. The band is not there to give easy answers and explanations but to inflict more doubts

---

[1] Fans of Pier Vittorio Tondelli, postmodern author and journalist.

and instil more insecurities to the audiences. This mechanism is typical of any other avant-garde especially in its beginning, with the difference that CCCP were doing this at the very end of the twentieth century, therefore also inheriting a confused, error-ridden, and diverse avant-garde heritage, in a Europe ridden by deindustrialization, experiencing processes of unification and pacification, and facing globalization, but still torn into two Blocs.

At the same time, popular music was expanding its creative possibilities beyond leisure and entertainment. To begin with, it was doing this from its English-speaking standpoint. Bands such as The Cure, Patti Smith Group, Bauhaus, and Joy Division and artists as Laurie Anderson were paradigm changers that affected music making all over the world, including, as seen, *Affinità e Divergenze*.

However, CCCP were also given a unique chance to transcend regional and national identities, balancing the local, the continental, and the international, while resisting cultural imperialism. They built their imaginary on off-modern European cultural memory, and by doing so, they created what we now in turn perceive as culture. The fact that the *Felicitazioni!* exhibition attracted 45,000 visitors (Montanari 2024) during its showing reveals that CCCP's work is perceived as cultural heritage, and its place is the stage and the museum alike.

Moreover, CCCP were provincial, just like bands as diverse as The Smiths, Fehlfarben, Marine Girls, UB40, Kleenex, VV, and Front 242. They did not come from a cultural capital and were not connected to art worlds and hegemonic cultural institutions. They were provincial intellectuals, who absorbed the twentieth century through paperbacks, film clubs, records, and newspapers and who were longing for a somewhere else that did not really exist.

Revisiting lesser-known albums, such as *Affinità e Divergenze*, shows that alternative cultural and musical heritages in Europe should make space to the provincial, outside the mere Anglo-American linguistic world, to fully make sense of how the last decades of the twentieth century absorbed the cultural memory of a tragic European century and turned it into something you could dance to without having to give up thinking.

# Bibliography

'1982 Ibanez Blazer Series Catalogue'. 1982. Accessed 25 September 2025. https://www.ibanez.com/usa/support/catalogs/.

Ahbe, Thomas. 2005. *Ostalgie: Zum Umgang Mit Der DDR-Vergangenheit in Den 1990er Jahren*. Erfurt: Landeszentrale für politische Bildung Thüringen.

Anderson, Ben. 2021. 'Affect and Critique: A Politics of Boredom'. *Environment and Planning D: Society and Space* 39 (2): 197–217.

Bagnasco, Arnaldo. 1977. *Tre Italie: la problematica territoriale dello sviluppo italiano*. Bologna: Il Mulino.

Ballico, Christina, ed. 2021. *Geographically Isolated and Peripheral Music Scenes: Global Insights and Perspectives*. Singapore: Springer.

Barilli, Renato. 2006. *Prima e Dopo Il 2000. La Ricerca Artistica 1970–2005*. Milano: Feltrinelli Editore.

Bianchi, Sandro Sench. 2024. Interview. 26 January 2024.

Bottà, Giacomo. 2018. 'Trying to Find a Clue, Trying to Find a Way to Get Out!: The European Imaginary of Joy Division'. In *Heart And Soul: Critical Essays On Joy Division*, edited by Martin J. Power, Eoin Devereux, and Aileen Dillane, 33–46. London: Rowman & Littlefield.

Bottà, Giacomo. 2020. *Deindustrialisation and Popular Music: Punk and 'Post-Punk' in Manchester, Düsseldorf, Torino and Tampere*. London: Rowman & Littlefield.

Bottà, Giacomo, and Ferruccio Quercetti. 2019. 'Brigade Rosse: The Clash, Bologna and Italian Punx'. In *Working for the*

*Clampdown: The Clash, the Dawn of Neoliberalism and the Political Promise of Punk*, edited by Colin Coulter, 209–22. Manchester: Manchester University Press.

Bottin, Guglielmo. 2024. 'Fedeli a Berlino. Influenze Della Neue Deutsche Welle Nel Post-Punk Emiliano Dei CCCP'. *La Rivista Di Engramma* (210). https://doi.org/10.25432/1826-901X/2024.210.0003.

Boyer, Dominic. 2006. 'Ostalgie and the Politics of the Future in Eastern Germany'. *Public Culture* 18 (2): 361–81.

Boym, Svetlana. 2017. *The Off-Modern*. New York: Bloomsbury.

Bratus, Alessandro. 2024. 'Ideologia Come Stile, Stile Come Ortodossia. La Costruzione Di Un Immaginario Spettacolare Nel Progetto Artistico Dei CCCP'. *La Rivista Di Engramma* (210). https://doi.org/10.25432/1826-901X/2024.210.0004.

Cámara de Landa, Enrique. 2002. 'Hybridization in the Tango Objects, Process, and Considerations'. In *Songs of the Minotaur – Hybridity and Popular Music in the Era of Globalization. A Comparative Analysis of Rebetika, Tango, Rai, Flamenco, Sardana, and English Urban Folk*, edited by Gerhard Steingress, 83–112. Münster: LIT.

Campo, Alberto, Ferretti, Giovanni Lindo, and Massimo Zamboni. 2005. *Fedeli alla linea. Dai CCCP ai CSI*. Florence, Italy: Giunti Editore.

Carroli, Laura. 2024. Interview. 15 March 2024.

Cavallo, Jo Ann. n.d. 'Epic Maggio | eBOIARDO'. Accessed 22 November 2024. https://edblogs.columbia.edu/eboiardo/epic-maggio/.

'CCCP – Fedeli Alla Linea – 1964–1985 Affinità-Divergenze Fra Il Compagno Togliatti E Noi Del Conseguimento Della Maggiore Età'. 1986. Accessed 25 September 2025. https://www.discogs.

com/master/119092-CCCP-Fedeli-Alla-Linea-1964-1985-Affinità-Divergenze-Fra-Il-Compagno-Togliatti-E-Noi-Del-Conseguime.

*CCCP – Fedeli Alla Linea – Live In Punkow*. 1996. Accessed 25 September 2025. https://www.discogs.com/master/1033567-CCCP-Fedeli-Alla-Linea-Live-In-Punkow.

Clementi, Emidio. 2024. Interview. 18 March 2024.

Contiero, Toni. 2015. *Fellegara. Dove sono nati i CCCP Fedeli alla linea. Ediz. illustrata*. Rimini: NFC Edizioni.

D'Alife, Luigi, and Andrea Paco Mariani, dirs. 2023. *Kissing Gorbaciov*. Documentary, Music. SMK Factory.

DAR – Dipartimento delle Arti, dir. 2021. *DAMS50 – Incontro Con Giovanni Lindo Ferretti*. Accessed 25 September 2025. https://www.youtube.com/watch?v=8b2GolDH4vw.

De Falchi, Edoardo, dir. 2023. 'Fedeli alla Linea: la linea non c'è | RaiPlay Sound'. *RaiPlaySound*. Accessed 25 September 2025. https://www.raiplaysound.it/programmi/fedelialinealinealalineanonce.

De Luca, Fabio. 2024. 'Message with Fabio De Luca'. 4 August 2024.

Demossier, Marion. 2016. 'The Europeanization of Terroir: Consuming Place, Tradition and Authenticity'. In *European Identity and Culture*, edited by Rebecca Friedman and Markus, Thiel, 119–36. Abingdon, Oxon; New York: Routledge.

Ercolino, Stefano. 2012. 'The Maximalist Novel'. *Comparative Literature* 64 (3): 241–56. https://doi.org/10.1215/00104124-1672925.

Esch, Rudi. 2016. *Electri_City: The Düsseldorf School of Electronic Music*. London: Omnibus Press.

Fatur, Danilo. 2023. Interview. 4 December 2023.

Ferretti, Giovanni Lindo, and Massimo Zamboni. 2022. *Il libretto rozzo*. Rome: GOG.

Fisher, Mark. 2022. *Capitalist Realism: Is There No Alternative?* Ropley: John Hunt Publishing.

Foot, John. 2015. *The Man Who Closed the Asylums: Franco Basaglia and the Revolution in Mental Health Care*. London; Brooklyn, NY: Verso.

Ganassini, Marcello. 2024. 'Messenger Exhange with Marcello Ganassini'. 31 January 2024.

Gasparini, Luca, dir. 1989. *Tempi Moderni. CCCP – Fedeli Alla Linea*. Accessed 25 September 2025. https://www.youtube.com/watch?v=sCmPNuCy4YU.

'"Geniale Dilletanten". Subkultur der 1980er-Jahre in Deutschland'. n.d. Haus der Kunst. Accessed 19 January 2024. https://www.hausderkunst.de/eintauchen/geniale-dilletanten-subculture-in-germany-in-the-1980s.

Ghiglione, Giorgio. 2022. '"It Takes Away My Melancholy": Liscio, the Glamorous Italian Club Scene for Older People'. *The Guardian*. Accessed 10 June 2022, sec. Music. https://www.theguardian.com/music/2022/jun/10/it-takes-away-my-melancholy-liscio-the-glamorous-italian-club-scene-for-older-people.

Giudici, Annarella, Giovanni Lindo Ferretti, and Rossana Tagliati. 2014. *Annarella benemerita soubrette: CCCP fedeli alla linea*. Macerata: Quodlibet.

Goldhammer, Rio. 2019. 'Provincial Towns and Yorkshire Cities: Post-Punk Sounds, Suburban Escape, and Metro-Hegemony'. In *Sounds and the City: Volume 2*, edited by Brett Lashua, Stephen Wagg, Karl Spracklen, and M. Selim Yavuz, 347–67. Cham: Springer International Publishing.

Golinowska, Karolina. 2016. 'Nostalgia for the PRL in Contemporary Poland'. *Twentieth Century Communism* 11 (11): 67–82. https://doi.org/10.3898/175864316819698512.

Gotor, Miguel. 2022. *Generazione Settanta: Storia Del Decennio Piú Lungo Del Secolo Breve 1966–1982*. Turin: Einaudi Storia. Einaudi.

Gramsci, Antonio. 1925. 'Massimalismo ed Estremismo'. *L'Unità*, 7 February 1925.

Haladyn, Julian Jason. 2015. *Boredom and Art: Passions of the Will to Boredom*. Ropley: John Hunt Publishing.

Hebdige, Dick. 2012. *Subculture: The Meaning of Style*. London: Routledge. https://doi.org/10.4324/9780203139943.

Hornberger, Barbara. 2011. *Geschichte Wird Gemacht: Die Neue Deutsche Welle; Eine Epoche Deutscher Popmusik*. Würzburg: Königshausen und Neumann.

Jameson, Fredric. 1991. *Postmodernism, Or The Cultural Logic of Late Capitalism*. Durham, NC: Duke University Press.

Kalinina, Ekaterina. 2014. 'Mediated Post-Soviet Nostalgia'. Accessed 25 September 2025. https://urn.kb.se/resolve?urn=urn:nbn:se:sh:diva-24576.

Krims, Adam. 2007. *Music and Urban Geography*. New York: Routledge.

Kromhout, Melle Jan, and Jan Nieuwenhuis. 2024. *Einstürzende Neubauten's Kollaps*. New York: Bloomsbury Academic.

Le Dinamiche, dir. 2023. *CCCP Fedeli Alla Linea Live – UfaFabrik Berlin 1985*. Accessed 25 September 2025. https://www.youtube.com/watch?v=pxY3A0BP6WY.

LeRoy, Dan. 2022. *Dancing to the Drum Machine: How Electronic Percussion Conquered the World*. New York: Bloomsbury Academic.

Lonkin, Claudia. 2024. *Neue Deutsche Welle*. New York: Bloomsbury Academic.

Maccioni, Germano, dir. 2013. *Fedele Alla Linea – Giovanni Lindo Ferretti*.

Massey, Doreen. 2005. *For Space*. London: SAGE.

Mendívil, Julio. 2016. 'Rocking Granny's Living Room? The New Voices of German Schlager'. In *Perspectives on German Popular Music*, edited by Michael Ahlers and Christoph Jacke. Abingdon, Oxon; New York: Routledge.

Mia Romagna. n.d. *Casadei Sonora Edizioni Musicali* (blog). Accessed 30 October 2024. https://www.casadeisonora.it/storia/romagna-mia/.

Micheli, Daniela, dir. 2011. *CCCP – Live in Fiorano, Circolo Titanic Estate 1983*. Accessed 25 September 2025. https://www.youtube.com/watch?v=-CijEF15hyw.

Mohr, Tim. 2018. *Burning Down the Haus: Punk Rock, Revolution, and the Fall of the Berlin Wall*. London: Hachette UK.

Montanari, Luca. 2024. 'Oltre 45mila visitatori alla mostra dei Cccp: "Non è ancora finita". VIDEO'. *Reggionline -Telereggio - Ultime notizie Reggio Emilia* (blog). Accessed 11 March 2024. https://www.reggionline.com/oltre-45mila-visitatori-la-mostra-dei-cccp-ferretti-sognare-fan-non-ancora-finita-video/.

Negri, Umberto. 2023a. Interview. 19 June 2023.

Negri, Umberto. 2023b. Interview. 22 June 2023.

Negri, Umberto. 2023c. *Io e i CCCP. Una storia fotografica e orale. Ediz. speciale*. Milan: ShaKe.

Ob&k, dir. 2015a. *Torino Paranoica: Band Bunker Club, Ferretti, Zamboni, Negri – CURAMI*. Accessed 25 September 2025. https://www.youtube.com/watch?v=Fc6ziAOEJmE.

Ob&k, dir. 2015b. *TORINO PARANOICA: Interviste a Giovanni Lindo Ferretti, Massimo Zamboni e Umberto Negri*. Accessed 25 September 2025. https://www.youtube.com/watch?v=tZlLp5lxw3A.

Ob&k, dir. 2015c. *Torino Paranoica: Losburla, Ferretti, Negri – TRAFITTO*. Accessed 25 September 2025. https://www.youtube.com/watch?v=vA0TiXB9nds.

Orlando, Ignazio. 2023. 'Messenger Message from Ignazio Orlando'. 9 November 2023.

Ottone, Lorenzo. 2021. 'When Bologna Was Italy's No Wave Capital: Tracing the Incendiary Story of Cult Band Gaznevada'. *Hero*. Accessed 2 August 2021. https://hero-magazine.com/article/184850/gazenevada.

Papa, Salvatore. 2024. 'Helena Velena (Che Scoprì i CCCP): «Danno Piazza Maggiore Ai Nazibolscevichi»'. Accessed 14 March 2024. https://zero.eu/en/news/helena-velena-che-scopri-i-cccp-danno-piazza-maggiore-ai-nazibolscevichi/.

Pécout, Christophe. 2016. 'La première scène punk en Normandie (1976–1980)'. *Volume !. La revue des musiques populaires* 13 (1) November: 31–45. https://doi.org/10.4000/volume.5021.

Plastino, Goffredo. 2023. *Rumore rosso: Patti Smith in Italia: rock e politica negli anni settanta*. Milan: Il Saggiatore.

Pustianaz, Maurizio. 2012. 'CCCP, 1985: come iniziarono gli stati di allucinazione – The New Noise'. Accessed 23 August 2012. https://www.thenewnoise.it/cccp-1985-iniziarono-gli-stati-di-allucinazione/,https://www.thenewnoise.it/cccp-1985-iniziarono-gli-stati-di-allucinazione/.

Reynolds, Simon. 2006. *Rip It up and Start Again: Postpunk 1978–1984*. New York : Penguin Books.

Richie, Alexandra. 1998. *Faust's Metropolis: A History of Berlin*. New York : Carroll & Graf.

Romania, Vincenzo. 2016. 'Fedeli Alla Linea: CCCP and the Italian Way to Punk'. *Revista Crítica de Ciências Sociais* 109 (May): 63–82. https://doi.org/10.4000/rccs.6215.

Rossi, Michele. 2024. '"Smettila Di Parlare, Avvicinati Un Po"'. Mi Ami? Dei CCCP – Fedeli Alla Linea'. *La Rivista Di Engramma* (210). https://doi.org/10.25432/1826-901X/2024.210.0008.

Stiglegger, Marcus. 2011. *Nazi-Chic und Nazi-Trash: faschistische Ästhetik in der populären Kultur*. Kultur & Kritik, ARRAY(0x55c70676d4c8). Berlin: Bertz + Fischer.

Tacchini, Alessandro. 1983. 'Intervista Ai CCCP Fedeli Alla Linea, 1983, Radio Antenna 1, Dj Alessandro Tacco Tacchini by Alessandro Tacco Tacchini | Mixcloud'. Accessed 25 September 2025. https://www.mixcloud.com/alessandro-tacco-tacchini/intervista-ai-cccp-fedeli-alla-linea-1983-radio-antenna-1-dj-alessandro-tacco-tacchini/.

Teil, Geneviève. 2011. 'No Such Thing as Terroir?'. *Science, Technology, & Human Values,* November. https://doi.org/10.1177/0162243911423843.

Teipel, Jürgen. 2001. *Verschwende Deine Jugend: ein Doku-Roman über den deutschen Punk und New Wave*. Berlin: Suhrkamp.

'Tens of Thousands of Italian Autoworkers Join First Strike in 20 Years – Newsweek'. n.d. Accessed 30 October 2024. https://www.newsweek.com/italian-autoworkers-union-strike-rome-1971404.

Terra, Bomba, dir. 2014. *CCCP Fedeli Alla Linea – Live al Festival Del Teatro 1983*. Accessed 25 September 2025. https://www.youtube.com/watch?v=SVfylyBuATo.

Terra, Bomba, dir. 2022. *CCCP Fedeli Alla Linea Emilia Paranoica – Live KOB 1983*. Accessed 25 September 2025. https://www.youtube.com/watch?v=3xKzeou818E.

'The Real Reason Nick Cave Moved to Berlin'. 2021. Accessed 17 November 2021. https://faroutmagazine.co.uk/the-real-reason-nick-cave-moved-to-berlin/.

Tomatis, Jacopo. 2021. *Storia culturale della canzone italiana*. Milan: Feltrinelli Editore.

Tondelli, Pier Vittorio. 2024. 'Punk, Falce e Martello'. *Linus* No. 2 Year 15.

Tosoni, Simone, and Emanuela Zuccalà. 2020. *Italian Goth Subculture: Kindred Creatures and Other Dark Enactments in Milan, 1982–1991*. Palgrave Studies in the History of Subcultures and Popular Music. Cham: Springer International Publishing.

Ubix, dir. 2012. *Benedetto Valdesalici – AHIMÈ Il Congresso Del Mondo – Con La Prima Apparizione Pubblica Dei CCCP*. Accessed 25 September 2025. https://www.youtube.com/watch?v=OJRUxvFR23E.

Velena, Helena. Interview. 22 March 2024.

Vinciullo, Francesca. 2015. 'Uno psichiatra punk rock: Intervista a Benedetto Valdesalici'. *State of Mind* (blog). Accessed 16 April 2015. https://www.stateofmind.it/2015/04/psichiatria-musica-benedetto-valdesalici/.

Volčič, Zala. 2007. 'Yugo-Nostalgia: Cultural Memory and Media in the Former Yugoslavia'. *Critical Studies in Media Communication* 24 (1): 21–38. https://doi.org/10.1080/07393180701214496.

Völker, Florian. 2023. 'Kälte-Pop: Die Geschichte des erfolgreichsten deutschen Popmusik-Exports'. In *Kälte-Pop*. De Gruyter Oldenbourg. https://doi.org/10.1515/9783111247090.

Worley, Matthew. 2020. '"I Don't Care about London": Punk in Britain's Provinces, circa 1976–1984'. In *The Oxford Handbook of Punk Rock*, edited by George McKay and Gina Arnold, 1st ed, 265–80. Oxford: Oxford University Press. https://doi.org/10.1093/oxfordhb/9780190859565.013.8.

Zamboni, Massimo. 2017. *Nessuna voce dentro: un'estate a Berlino Ovest*. Turin: Einaudi.

Zarucchi, Max, dir. 2021. *CCCP Fedeli Alla Linea – Sky, Soliera (MO), Italy*. Accessed 7 November 2025. https://www.youtube.com/watch?v=n8X8zLaF4Rs.

Zarucchi, Max. 2025. 'CCCP: affinità e divergenze tra i Fedeli alla linea e noi Come eravamo (così carini)'. Humans vs Robots. Accessed 5 May 2025. https://hvsr.net/post/2025/cccp-affinita-e-divergenze-tra-i-fedeli-alla-linea-e-noi.

Zuffanti, Fabio. 2021. 'Gaznevada, gli outsider della Bologna punk diventati classici | Rolling Stone Italia'. *Rolling Stone Italia*. Accessed 24 January 2021. https://www.rollingstone.it/musica/interviste-musica/gaznevada-gli-outsider-della-bologna-punk-diventati-classici/548027/.

# Index

1977 Movement 40–1
*77* (nickname) 72

Abwärts (band) 20
Adam and the Ants (band) 68
agitprop 15
*AHIMÈ il congresso del mondo* (film) 29–31
Arno (artist) 9
Atonal (festival) 25–6
Attack Punk Records 38, 52

Barthes, Roland 62
Basaglia, Franco 30
Bauhaus (band) 70, 95
Berlin 13–27, 48, 58–60, 80–3
Berlin clubs 20
Bianchi, Sandro aka Sench 41–2
Bologna 38–43
Bonvicini, Silvia 49, 55, 68–9, 72, 86
Boredom 67–9
Boym, Svetlana 89
BRD, FRG, Federal Republic of Germany 16, 18

C.S.I. (Consorzio Suonatori Indipendenti) 9
Carpi 29, 35, 38
Carroli, Laura 38–9, 42, 50
Casiotone VL-1 49
CCCP band logo 37

Chiapparini, Carlo aka Bounty Scarponacci 38, 50, 54, 72
Cimar 2072 MH (basso) 49
Clementi, Emidio 92–3
Cold War 19, 61
cold-pop 18–19
compagni, cittadini, fratelli, partigiani (EP) 6, 70

DAF (band) 22, 61
DAMS (Drama, Art and Music Studies) 21, 40, 62
Das Rote Sprachrohr (band) 15
DDR, GDR, German Democratic Republic 16–17
De Luca, Fabio 61–2, 94
*Die große Untergangs-Show – Festival Genialer Dilletanten* 22
Die Toten Hosen (band) 9

East Berlin 16, 22, 81
Eastern Bloc 17, 80–3
Einstürzende Neubauten (band) 9, 19, 22
Električni Orgazam (band) 9
Emilia-Romagna 27, 37
ethnomusicology 22, 29, 40

Fatur, Danilo aka Josè Lopez Macho Frasquelo 16, 26–7, 35, 54, 63, 92
Fehlfarben (band) 67

*Felicitazioni!* (exhibition and anniversary events) 80, 95
Fellegara 1–6, 71, 77, 84
Ferretti, Giovanni Lindo 3, 7–8, 21, 25–6, 29–30, 39–40, 56, 60, 63, 65, 71, 84, 88
Flux of Pink Indians (band) 43
Fostex (8-track, 16-track recorder) 51
Frigo (band) 24, 46

Ganassini, Marcello 94
Gaznevada (band) 43
Geniale Dilletanten 19, 22, 24
Giudici, Annarella 9, 16, 26–7, 53, 59, 63, 68, 83, 86
Giudici, Zeo 23, 29, 45, 63–4
Gramsci, Antonio 86
*grattuggiare* 57

harmonica 49, 56–7

Ibanez Blazer BL500 (guitar) 49
Indochine (band) 9
Italian Communist Party (PCI) 7, 28, 31, 40, 55–6
Italian punk 35, 42–3, 87, 94
Italian Records 43, 50

KGB 57
Korg KPR77 (drum machine) 46
Kuhle Wampe, oder: Wem gehört die Welt? (film) 14

Laibach (band) 9
*Legge 180* (law) 30
Leydi, Roberto 40

liscio 37, 64–5
Lonkin, Claudia 18
Lotta Continua 41

*Maggio Drammatico* 28
Massey, Doreen 76
maximalism / minimalism 84–7
maximalism 86
melodica 49, 69–70
metallophone 49, 59
Mitropa 23
MitropaNK 23–7
Morselli, Mirca 25–6, 32, 45

Negri, Umberto 2, 24, 26, 29, 32, 46, 49, 57, 64, 73
Neue Deutsche Welle (NDW) 17–19
No Wave 43, 57
Nuovi-nuovi 58

Oberheim DMX 48–9
off-modern (theory) 87–9
Orlando, Ignazio 48, 50, 72
*Ortodossia* (EP) 1, 6, 31
*Ortodossia II* (EP) 6, 32, 37, 60
Ostalgie 7, 80–4

Pianura Padana 2, 4–5
postmodern / post-modern theory 82, 88
provincia / provinciality 4, 8, 33–6, 77–80
punk and post-punk 5, 8–9, 15, 42, 70

Reggio Emilia 1, 27–30, 34, 85

reverb (studio effect) 51
Reynolds, Simon 8, 91
Rondos (band) 39

Santarcangelo di Romagna 31–3
*Schlager* 65
Smith, Patti (singer) 5, 70
soprano sax 49
Soviet iconography 27, 37
Soviet Union 17, 55, 81
squat 20, 35, 58, 60, 72
*Stampa Alternativa* 26
Superfluo (studio) 50–1

techno 16, 20, 22
territorialization (imaginary and affective) 7, 37, 80
terroir 76–7
*Terza Italia* 28
The Cure (band) 56, 59, 70
Togliatti, Palmiro 54–5

Tuwat 35, 72, 85
twee 62

UFA Fabrik 83
UK Subs (band) 63

Valium, Tavor, Serenase, Plegine, Rohypnol (drugs) 64, 72
Velena, Helena aka Giampaolo 'Jumpy' Giorgetti 38, 43, 53
Virgin records 6, 9, 50, 52

West Berlin 13, 20, 23–4, 83
Wolfango, Üstmamó, Marlene Kuntz (bands emerging via CPI / 1990s) 9

Yamaha RX11, RX5 (drum machines) 48

Zamboni, Massimo 19, 32, 36, 43, 46, 49, 57–8, 60, 66, 71